Philo's Reply

To Questions Concerning His Association

With the Illuminati

© 2012 Jeva Singh-Anand.

ISBN 978-1-105-60407-2

Translated from German

Original Title:

Philo's endliche Erklaerung und Antwort auf verschiedene Anforderungen und Fragen die an ihn ergangen, seine Verbindung mit dem Orden der Illuminaten betreffend

by Freiherr Adolph Franz Friedrich Ludwig Knigge

1788

Cover Illustration:

Adolph Freiherr Knigge

(public domain)

First Edition, 2012

Freiherr Adolph Franz Friedrich Ludwig Knigge
(1752-1796):

In the German speaking world, "Knigge" is a household word that has become synonymous with etiquette, largely due to his three volume treatise *Practical Philosophy of Social Life or, The Art of Conversing with Men*, still a standard reference on the subject. However, Knigge was a prolific writer whose work covers a broad spectrum of topics in the social sciences and humanities.

Born into lesser nobility, Knigge developed a nearly lifelong fascination with occult sciences and secret societies, which he abandoned later in life for theological and humanistic pursuits. He studied law in Göttingen, Germany and joined Strict Observance, a Masonic Lodge in Cassel, in 1772. During his efforts to reform and streamline Freemasonry, he joined the Bavarian Illuminati in 1780. As the de facto second in command of the order's founder, Adam Weishaupt, he expanded the Illuminati's influence exponentially and fully developed the order's degree system. Following a bitter dispute with Weishaupt, he left the Illuminati in 1784. Knigge died in 1796 after a prolonged illness.

About the Translator:

Born in Hamburg, Germany, Jeva Singh-Anand is a freelance translator and writer. He received his Masters in English degree in 1997. A former public school teacher and corporate trainer, Singh-Anand has published a collection of short stories, a one-act play, and numerous articles on a wide variety of topics.

A skeptic on the subject of conspiracy theories, he has nonetheless cultivated an intense fascination with the historical Bavarian Illuminati and the original documents surrounding this legendary secret society.

Singh-Anand has traveled to four continents. He lived in the Pacific Rim for two years, where he became an avid Scuba-enthusiast. He currently lives in Iowa with his two sons.

Translator's Foreword

Philo's Reply to Questions Concerning His Association with the Illuminati is interesting in several aspects. For one, it offers important and unexpected insights into the history and structure of the Bavarian Illuminati as well as Freemasonry that are not widely known outside the Masonic community. It also contains a brief autobiographical sketch of one of Germany's most important thinkers and writers of the 1700s, Baron Adolph Franz Friedrich Ludwig Knigge (1752-1796), who expanded the Bavarian Illuminati exponentially under the assumed name Philo and adjusted this secret society to the Freemasonic system in order to unite and influence the Freemasonic community. In this brief work, Knigge furthermore renders an insightful character sketch of the Illuminati's founder, Adam Weishaupt as well as his own narrative of the events leading to the falling out between

Weishaupt and Knigge and his subsequent resignation from the Illuminati.

During his short life, Adolph Knigge was a prolific writer with a restless, inquisitive mind. To the German speaking world, he is best known for his three volume anthropological treatise *Practical Philosophy of Social Life or, The Art of Conversing with Men* (1788), which has curiously been popularized as a standard work on etiquette. Growing up in his family's household, there was frequent conversation about mystic subjects and secret societies. These conversations had such a powerful impression on the young Knigge, that as a school boy, he banded together with a few classmates and formed a secret society of his own. He wrote,

> I attached a silver cross to a thread and looped it through a button hole, and with several other young men, drew up laws on a half sheet of paper, which were more innocent – to say the least – and certainly no

less effective than the laws of some larger secret societies[1].

His fascination with secret societies would later lead him into Freemasonry, where he joined the Strict Observance Lodge in Cassel. His financial circumstances and rebellious nature prevented him from progressing in the lodge as quickly as he desired. His move to Hanau in 1777 proved to be more fortunate in this respect. The local baron was in the process of establishing a new lodge. He was eager to promote the few Masons scattered throughout the town in order to fill up the necessary, vacant lodge offices. It was his involvement in Freemasonry and his desire to unite Masonry for the purpose of the betterment of humanity that led to Knigge's involvement with the Bavarian Illuminati.

The Illuminati cannot be called an ancient organization by any standard, and until Knigge's

---

[1] Knigge, 1788

involvement, they were a rather insignificant organization. Leopold Engel, in *Geschichte des Illuminaten-Ordens*[2], dates the foundation of the order to May 1, 1776. The order was founded by Adam Weishaupt, a professor of canon law at the University of Ingolstadt, Bavaria, to counter the influence of the recently disbanded, but still powerful Jesuits in the Bavarian educational system. When in 1780 Knigge made the acquaintance of the Marquis de Constanza, known as Diomedes among the Illuminati, he was disillusioned with the state of Freemasonry in the German states and frustrated by his own efforts to unite the various lodges under a common, greater cause.

"I am resolved to develop a new system with a circle of trusted, good brothers, scattered throughout Germany," he told the Marquis[3]. Knigge was resolved to approach a select few

---

[2] Tr. *The History of the Order of the Illuminati*
[3] Knigge, 1788

Masons whom he trusted to join him in his effort to unify and redirect Freemasonry. It was then that the Marquis revealed to him that such an organization already existed.

"Why waste your efforts to create something new," the Marquis replied. "When there is a society that has already accomplished what you seek and which is able to satisfy your thirst for knowledge and your eagerness to be active and useful; a society that is powerful and educated enough to do and teach everything you demand?[4]"

In the further course of this conversation, the Marquis de Constanza, who was on a mission to recruit members in the Germany's Protestant states, claimed that this secret society, The Order of Bavarian Illuminati had been responsible for the large scale proliferation of Enlightenment Philosophy throughout the courts of the German

---

[4] Knigge, 1788

states. Knigge enthusiastically petitioned for membership and was soon accepted.

His first task was to recruit new members and to set up seed schools in five districts in the German states. He soon found himself the victim of his own success. In his districts, the Order of Illuminati soon swelled to several hundred members, and he found that administering these districts – and delivering on the promises he made his recruits – became a nearly impossible mission.

Adam Weishaupt painted a picture in the most brilliant colors when he described the Illuminati,

> a society, which by the finest and most secure means achieves the goal, to ensure the victory of virtue and wisdom over folly in the world, to achieve the most important discoveries in all areas of science, to mold its members into noble and great persons, and to ensure certain rewards even in this world for their perfection, to protect them from persecution, ill fate, and oppression, and tie the hands of any kind of despotism[5].

---

[5] Knigge, 1788

Weishaupt promised nothing less than Heaven on earth to the members of this secret society, who in financial, political, and spiritual security would work for the enlightenment and liberation of humankind. Backed by Weishaupt's word of honor, Knigge presented the order's goals and influence in even more glowing terms, "Where [Weishaupt] promised Elysium, I, true to my temper, promised Paradise[6]."

Delivering on these promises, however, was easier said than done.

Knigge was now in charge of several hundred students, and since he had not advanced to any of the higher degrees in the order, he was not in a position to install subordinate leaders who could have shared his weighty load. When he wrote to Weishaupt that the seed schools under his care were in danger of falling apart, for a variety of

---

[6] Knigge, 1788

reasons, Weishaupt revealed at last his great secret,

> The order does not yet exist, only in my mind. Only the lower class, the seed school has been established in a few Catholic Provinces; but I have assembled the most magnificent materials *en masse* for the higher degrees. Would you forgive my little fraud? I have long yearned to find worthy collaborators for this great work, but have found none, other than you, who penetrate into the spirit of the system as deeply as I do and is so conscientiously and tirelessly active[7].

Weishaupt promised to send his materials to Knigge, so that he could develop these degrees. He also invited Knigge to travel to Bavaria so he could meet with the other leaders of the order, the Areopagites. This revelation placed Knigge into a rather peculiar dilemma. He had been working under the assumption that the Illuminati were a well-established organization whose degree system was already in existence. He had not imagined he

---

[7] Knigge, 1788

would be tasked with developing it himself. Seeing the progress his own Provinces had made, keeping in mind the promises he had made his subordinates, and admiring Weishaupt's vision and tireless zeal, he was resolved not to abandon the work. He agreed to travel to Bavaria, meet with Weishaupt and the Areopagites and develop the higher degrees for the Order of Illuminati.

Knigge's system included three classes, the seed school, Masonry, and the Mysteries. Each class was divided into two subsections. The seed school, divided into Novitiates and Minervals, was designed to introduce students to the philosophical principles of the order and to ensure that these students were sufficiently receptive to its mission. The Freemasons and Regents were the order's business arm and administrators, while the Mysteries Class was dedicated to educating the students and to engage in speculative thought. Knigge elaborated, the Minervals were to be pupils and students; the Freemasons, educated, worldly men and businessmen; the priests, scholars and teachers; the regents, leaders and directors; and finally, the members of the Higher Mysteries degrees, speculative seers, who had withdrawn into a philosophical retirement after they had been active in the world long enough[8].

The Greater Mysteries class was to be put off until the order was more established, according to an agreement with Weishaupt and the Areopagites. While Knigge was a member of the Illuminati, these were never developed.

There has been much talk about the Illuminati's supposedly evil intentions. Weishaupt in his pamphlet, *A Brief Justification Of My Intentions To Illuminate The Latest Original Writings*, vehemently defended the order's philanthropic goals, stating that an impartial reader could find nothing in the Illuminati documents, which had been published by order of the electoral

---

[8] Knigge, 1788

government in Munich, was dangerous or pernicious[9]. Even Knigge defended the Illuminati's aims, despite the fact that he had not left the order on good terms. In his description of the Priest degree, which closely draws from the mysteries of the Christian faith, he outlined them as follows:

> to raise humanity back to its original dignity; to raise morality to its highest degree through wise education; to introduce a general regimen of morals, so that anyone could remain faithful to virtuousness from his inner conviction that only virtue can bring happiness, without coercion; to bind all people to one another with the bonds of brotherhood; to remove all immediate conditions causing poverty, need, and the fight against depravity and immorality by enabling us to govern ourselves and consequently do without all artificial institutions, constitutions and positive laws[10].

The goals, according to Knigge, were to raise humanity through education to a moral and

---

[9] Weishaupt, 1787
[10] Knigge, 1788

spiritual condition, in which human beings could govern themselves without artificial constraints and laws, and poverty, crime, and immorality would disappear. In other words, he proposed a system that would nonviolently lead to the elimination of all systems. It was a paradox with which he was never fully at ease, and later in life, he lost all interest in secret societies and systems whatsoever.

Adam Weishaupt was, according to Knigge, a driven, honorable, and intelligent man. However, he was also difficult to work with. He was well respected by the citizens of his hometown Ingolstadt, Bavaria, living a modest, morally impeccable life, and he conducted his business affairs faithfully. He enjoyed a reputation of scholarliness and wisdom among his peers. Knigge admired him as a profound thinker, whose brilliant mind was always hungry for knowledge that was not easily available in Bavaria. To a large extent, the Bavarian education system was still firmly in the grip of former members of the then disbanded Jesuit order. It was not easy to obtain academic books by non-Catholic authors or books that were at odds with the doctrines of the Roman Catholic Church[11]. His tireless, selfless dedication for the greater cause and the Illuminati was, Knigge speculated, spurred by Weishaupt's sense of self-worth.

On the other hand, while Weishaupt was able to overcome great obstacles with strength and courage, insignificant bickering and minor obstacles tended to discourage him. He was also a man who demanded strict obedience. The Areopagites, who were at odds with Weishaupt during Knigge's visit to Bavaria, complained that he was despotic and fickle. They stated

> He believes himself to be chief of all men, a Messiah, and treats no one with justice, only those who flatter him. Such a man he elevates to the Heavens for a while. However, a minor circumstance, a

---

[11] Engel, 1906

> lack of blind devotion to his whims, can lower the noblest man in his esteem, while on the other hand a little a little cow-towing and homage will assure even the most crooked head his unlimited trust[12].

Knigge ascribed these flaws to Weishaupt's Jesuit upbringing, his sense of self-worth escalating into egomania as the order suddenly expanded in size and influence, and his all-consuming dedication to the order. However, even his admiration for Weishaupt as a thinker and philanthropist was not sufficient to prevent the schism between the two men that would ultimately lead to Knigge's resignation from the Illuminati in 1783.

When Knigge traveled to Bavaria to meet with Weishaupt and the Areopagites, he was given the task to develop the order's degree system. According to the written agreement between the parties, Knigge's drafts of the degrees were to be reviewed by the Areopagites, then approved and

---

[12] Knigge, 1788

further revised by Weishaupt and after they were distributed to the lodges, further revisions were only to be made during a subsequent convention of the Illuminati. Knigge had to wait for a long time to hear back from the Areopagites after he submitted the drafts, and when he complained to Weishaupt, Weishaupt replied, "The whole thing must not be held back by the slothfulness of these persons. Please institute these degrees as you have designed them without giving it a second thought[13]."

However, soon after these degrees were distributed to the Illuminati lodges, Weishaupt sent revisions to Knigge with the demand that they be instituted at once. Knigge replied that this not only violated the agreement all parties had signed in Bavaria, but also pointed out that this process involved significant logistical problems – as all degrees had to be copied by hand and properly authenticated – and furthermore was indicative of

---

[13] Knigge, 1788

a weak, inconsistent government that could call the order's integrity into question. These arguments did not impress Weishaupt in the least, and he insisted on absolute obedience. A bitter factional quarrel ensued, and Knigge saw no other choice than to withdraw from the order altogether.

The reader must decide for himself, whether the Illuminati, as Knigge described them, were a sinister or benevolent organization. Knigge himself, though he never was at odds with the order's aims, ultimately became disillusioned with secret societies altogether. However, his influence on the order's organization and proliferation cannot be denied.

Sioux City, Iowa, 2012

Bibliography:

Engel, Leopold. *Geschichte des Illuminaten-Ordens*. Berlin. Hugo Bermuehler Verlag. 1906

Knigge, Adolph. *Philo's Reply to Questions Concerning His Involvement with the Illuminati*. (Lulu). 2012

Weishaupt, Adam. A Brief Justification of my Intentions to Illuminate the Latest Original Writings. 1787

Philo's Reply to Questions

Concerning His Association with the Illuminati

A man has to put up with many things this day and
age. The spirit of spying out and anecdote-
collecting becomes more commonplace every day;
under the protection of press-freedom and the
public's right to know, one has taken the liberty of
casting a probing light on every step a man may
take within his own four walls, on every private
letter, and every word he may speak within a circle
of close friends, so one may publicly chastise every
little indiscretion of which he may be guilty and
hold him responsible for all these things; without
any knowledge of the issues, nameless persons
publicize their final analyses of matters they do not
understand; boys piece together reviews of the
works of great men which are then printed as a
scholarly word of force by their schoolmaster's
publishing house; the literary and moral
highwayman drags the murderer in front of the

court of his gang of thieves, and the heretic pulls the mantle of the Dominicans over his shoulders to play the main character in an *auto da fe*.

When, as all too often, in this course an unfounded suspicion is pinned to an innocent man in the eyes of the weaker part of the public, and his character is cast in a false light, as soon it behooves such an Anonymous – out of wrongness or malice – to write an irritating fairy tale and send it out into the world, or he demands from such a man explanations he cannot give without bringing embarrassment to himself and others even when he is fully aware of his innocence; but even so, this tone may cause more benefit than injury. The public retains its ability to distinguish between innocence and libel, between just accusations and unjust persecutions. The fear of being spied out and brought into the public light may at least curb some types of frauds and villains as well as some, who could or have carelessly caused harm, and teach that one must speak and act with caution. It is good that a person should pay a small penance for his folly. An honest confession does not lessen the penitent in the eyes of noble and honest persons, and as a matter of principle, he must be indifferent to the judgment of the others. But he, who is ashamed to make such a confession, deserves to be rapped across the knuckles, and he also deserves the distrust of those who may believe this was not his last act of foolishness. It would also be very healthy, if as a rule, as little as possible were done in secret. Few good intentions need to fear the light; few sensible sentences that have been proliferated in secret are in need of secrecy, and few good deeds done in secret need to remain a secret forever. There are few things that cannot be explained, no matter how complicated they may be; or at least, they can be clarified in such a manner, that the public can be satisfied there is no knavery at work, even when it must be taken into consideration, that certain things are impossible to break them down to the smallest parts. This is especially the case when the man involved has earned respectability and a general good report in his private life. In the end, the villain reveals himself; treacherous and rank enemies enmesh themselves in the web of their own malicious deeds; the truth will see the light of day, it triumphs, and does not remain distorted; time reveals everything and repels the apparatus of impassioned blinding mirrors and prejudices. Indeed, I would to remind the reader of many arguments against the other side of anonymity inasmuch as documents do not replace the accuser's missing name—but this is not the place for it. It is not my purpose to argue for or against the freedom of the press or the public's right to know. I only wanted to write these introductory remarks to address the reason that has moved me to present these pages to the public.

During my connection with the Illuminati, various events came to pass, which intimately concerned my person, causing members, some in this order and some in other secret societies, to feel entitled to demand explanations from me. I gave these explanations as long as I considered it right and well with respect to persons and property, reason, honor, and usefulness and as long as doing so was not in contradiction with my obligations. At times, when idle banter put me in an ill mood; when I learned in the course of such actions that others, who had been sworn to secrecy, in their talkativeness had much to say to the profane public regarding my relationship with the Illuminati; when men, whom I had reason to consider impartial and wise, exhorted me to put an end to this idle chatter; in those times, I did feel a small urge to make a public appearance and present the true side of the matter; it was only thanks to sensible friends and cool-headed reason that I did not do this. I am a free man, and I do not beg protection, charity, or favor of any man on

God's green earth. Nor do I demand of any man more than what could be asked of justice and good, free will with good cause—What did I care, if I pleased this or that man, who believed himself more important than he appeared to me as he scrutinized[i] me through his opera glasses? What did I care, if someone whom I did not know held me in high regard or not; if someone who did not know the inner workings of the Order of the Illuminati or myself, or both combined, had a proper understanding of these things or not? By and by, the whole matter went away, and since four years after having left this secret society, I have heard nearly nothing of it, I hardly gave these irksome ramblings which had been directed at me, any further thought.

However the matter appeared to assume an entirely different character, when the *Original Writings of the Illuminati*, plus the postscript to the same, published by the order of the electoral government in Munich, the entire public, by presenting it with documents proving the supposedly dangerous nature of the Illuminati, was at once invited to pass judgment on the entire order. I had been their co-leader, eager benefactor and – later – a dissatisfied member under the name Philo, as a large number of people knew.

It is true that I could expect that impartial persons who did not know the order very well, other than what they saw in these original writing, would first ask the following questions before deciding anything:

1. Are these indeed authentic documents, documents on which the system of the Illuminati is based? Do they contain the true principles on which this entire secret society acted, or are these perhaps only personal opinions, the private papers of individual members, that prove nothing against the society as a whole? Sketches, essays submitted and copied by members? Suggestions?
2. Are they complete, or perhaps abridged?
3. What is meant when the electoral commissioners say: these letters were written in Spartacus' or Philo's or Cato's own hand? Certainly not by the Lacedemonic legislator Spartacus? Not by the philosophical Philo? Etc. In other words, by those in the order who assumed the names of the ancients? And who exactly are they? Do we know them for certain? And if I am this Philo, who will vouch that this so-called Philo's handwriting is my own? How would the commissioners know my handwriting?

4. Where the accused interrogated properly? Did they verify these documents, their authenticity, completeness, and the handwriting?

These and several other related questions remain to be asked, and to tell the truth, the more judicious part of the public has been thoughtful enough to refrain from passing judgment, until several of the order's superiors personally appeared, defended themselves and the good cause, admitted some of their errors, and saved the society's honor.

On this occasion, I was urged again to do the same, and since (if one does not think as the masses do) there is no shortage of little men who are all too eager to pin a tail on me, no matter how much I'd like to walk my own life quietly and peacefully, it so happened that I learned from my friends that people from various backgrounds have spent idle hours finding whatever they could to ascribe in these original writings to Philo so they could cast my reputation in an evil, suspicious light. But I still did not deem it necessary to make a public appearance, because:

1. I was not mentioned by name; why should I be the first to admit to these letters, published without any proof of authenticity and written

under an assumed name? It would have been counterproductive, because I only would have drawn the attention of those who did not yet know who Philo was?

2. Impartial persons found nothing in Philo's letters with which any honest man could have been criminally charged, and I unabashedly challenge any man who loves the truth, who has not been blinded by partisanship, to show me anything of the sort in these letters. I do not think it is a criminal act that a man expresses certain opinions at some point in time (which me may have later abandoned and corrected) without weighing every single word about individuals, state constitutions, religious systems, other orders and so forth in his personal letters which were not intended for publication, to a friend, which he was duty bound to do, in order to come to an agreement as to how to influence these matters and persons.

3. Those persons who were cast in a less favorable light were in a better position to plead their own causes.

4. Neither did I feel a calling to become the order's apologist. This was Herr Weishaupt's place, who had let it publicly be known that he was the order's founder.

5. Since it was known that I had completely left the order four years ago, it seemed indulgent and philanthropic to believe that (were the order governed by dangerous principles and plans) I probably left it because I could no longer in good conscience participate in these matters, although this is not the case, as will be seen in the following pages.

6. I thought it immodest to further tire the public with more such writings, and no one challenged me to do so publicly and by name. I do not like to answer, if I am not asked; he who asks me under four eyes, to him I will answer under four eyes, and I pay no attention to idle gossip.

7. When I left the order, I had sworn secrecy, had promised not to name any of the superiors, nor compromise them, and without this, my defense would have remained incomplete. Therefore, I could not make a needless appearance until I was convinced I would not reveal anything that was not already known, but only needed to explain that which was known.

8. Further, I knew that the judgment of the just was on my side, and in my unencumbered position, I do not lust after the applause of the weak-minded crowd.

9. And certainly, it is proof that among the order's documents were no truly dangerous things written by my hand, that when the persecution of the Illuminati and Freemasons was in full progress, I lived quietly and unmolested in Palatinate, then left that beautiful country without having received the slightest request in the matter by the electoral government.

These were the reasons I chose to not entangle myself in this matter, but I did pay attention to these writings which were published regarding this matter. My person was not referenced in a single one of these, even in Herr Stark's postscript to his thick volume, although he often cites passages from Philo's letters.

An honest and generous person by any standard shines through Herr Nicolai's public explanation regarding his secret connection with the Order of the Illuminati. In complete truthfulness, he declared his secret connection with the order, but other than Herr Weishaupt, he did not name a single member, including me.

The Baron of Bassus, on the other hand, mentions my name on several occasions in his printed presentation to the heads of state of the Republic of Grisons[ii]. He does so in a manner that befits his loveable character, but by introducing me to the public as Philo, he has put me in a position where I do have say a word about myself, and as I pick up my quill, I see yet another newspaper challenging me to do just that.

So be it, then! I will tell the story of my connection with the Order of the Illuminati here, and I hope to convince the impartial at least reader of the innocence of my intentions in all things I effected there. This will cast some notable passages (which I gladly authenticate as Philo's letters, reports, etc.) in a milder light. It will even, I flatter myself, strengthen the good opinions sympathetic persons may have of the order and its members in general. I wish to speak modestly of myself and with suitable restraint as far as others are concerned, not keep my own mistakes secret, nor enlarge those of others – this is how we arrive at the goal!

From my youth, I was spurred on by an unquiet drive, which I could only later channel into temperate, useful limits, and so I also was stricken with our era's great disease at an early age: a yearning for secret connections and orders. Even as a child in my father's house, I heard enthusiastic talk about Freemasonry and the secret sciences, because it was then that it became all the rage, and my father, who certainly never managed to create gold, was nonetheless often surrounded by persons who spoke about the philosopher's stone and similar matters. As a boy, I attached a silver cross to a thread and looped it through a button hole, and with several other young men, drew up laws on a half sheet of paper, which were more innocent – to say the least – and certainly no less effective than the laws of some larger secret societies. As a university student, I belonged to an order that harbored quite a few laudable intentions, but whose plans were not designed with the same degree of thoroughness with which one would hammer them out, now that my experiences in this area have increased so manifold. I also joined a few joined a few smaller ladies orders – and all these pacts finally stirred within me an ardent desire for Freemasonry, which according to my judgment – right or wrong, but that is neither here nor there – kept important secret knowledge, because it had been in existence for so long, and so many of the best and most knowledgeable people had preoccupied themselves with it.

As soon as I had reached the required minimum age, I entered the Lodge of the Strict Observance in Cassel in the year 1772. At the time, it was led by an honorable man who valued culture, order, submission, and morals among the members, as well as punctual payment of the prescribed membership dues. My sauciness, youth (I was not yet 20 years old), lack of a subordinate spirit, poor conditions at home, and my then peculiar political circumstances kept me from advancing in the order; I remained an apprentice. This was an insult to my vanity, which would have loved to see me play a more important role. To make up for my lack of lawfully acquired knowledge, I decided to do some research. *The Freemason Betrayed* and similar books provided me with the material, as did a traitor who was well-versed in the system of the Strict Observance, in other words: a Templar, told me over a bottle of wine the arrangements of all degrees in this system, and he did not neglect to raise within me ambitious speculations about the hidden masters and clerics. Proud of the new treasure trove of knowledge, I intended to cash in on the same and to thus force my advance in the order free of charge; this only had the effect (regardless of the fact that, as far as the development of Freemasonry was concerned, the establishment of the Order of the Knights Templar was a great secret) that this was completely disregarded, that I was told this knowledge was true, but to divulge it or not at my own risk, that I should seek advancement the usual way or otherwise fail; I found myself somewhat insulted by this, and consequently visited the lodge only rarely.

In the year 1777, I moved to Hanau. When under the protection of a very eager baronial Brother, a lodge was established, and he sought to unite the few Freemasons scattered throughout that small town in order to fill all offices, I also was considered. My current relations at the court and the promise I was given, to quickly advance through the degrees of the system, but to leave payment of the reception fees to my leisure, moved me to tackle the matter once more in all seriousness, and I did so in my own manner and with burning eagerness. Thus, I achieved acceptance into the higher order, of which I certainly had knowledge, under the name *a cygno*, and now I proceeded, so as to not embark on it half-heartedly, to study the much-praised higher sciences.

I had no particular occupation (apart from directing a few insignificant theater plays); was full of drive; thirsty for wisdom; not satisfied by the conventional philosophical systems; at an age, where the establishment and destruction of a philosophical school comes easiest; tickled by the vain idea to occupy myself with higher matters than other, common people, to play a grand role in the world of Freemasonry and thus gain influence in the bourgeois society, in which – apart from a circle of a few miles – I was a rather insignificant person; and as far as religion was concerned, I floated between faith and disbelief, was dissatisfied with the church-systems, not assuaged by the mere cult of reason, filled with doubt regarding a few revealed sentences, full of yearning for a better, supernatural illumination. The higher degrees of the Strict Observance pointed so clearly in that direction; thus I thought it very probable that so many learned and noble-minded adherents to this system would not limit themselves to such a small and trivial purpose as restoring the outer luster of an ancient knightly order; but that, when they engaged in such child's play, more exalted matters would occur in the background. Old manuscripts passed through my hands; I had the opportunity to learn about the higher degrees, very rare degrees, of other Masonic branches – everything led to secret, higher sciences. I made the acquaintance of the Blessed Schroeder in Marburg, who would have been able to inspire an interest in Theosophy, magic and alchemy in even the coolest intellects – and I was not a cool-headed man, but a very warm-blooded, fantastical, and blustering youth of twenty-five years. Greedily, I embarked on my adventures; wherever there was a house where the maid or a servant, or both, were plagued by an evil spirit; wherever a clever monk was said to cite the spirits of the dead and conjure forth shadows from the graves; wherever an old man lived in seclusion from the world, luring gullible fools to his melting pots – the honorable Brother *a cygno* was not far.

Soon I earned a reputation of practicing this mystic trade myself, and this reputation followed me to Frankfurt on the Main, where I moved in the year 1780 – indeed! especially my solitary way of life strengthened this opinion among the faithful. And no practicing ghost-seer, high or low, no travelling hunter of mysteries, no begging maker of gold could pass up my house. My garden house had a turret. One of the Craft who visited me, quipped, "This is the tower in which you do your celestial work."

I never practiced alchemy very much; as far as I can remember, half a dozen silver coffee spoons is all I used for it. But I quickly memorized the jargon of these mystics; I half-believed, half-doubted; in part, I was deceived and seduced, but in part, I deceived and seduced others – not to defraud them, but to avoid betraying my own lack of knowledge in these matters and not to scare away the masters of these arts, with whose help I hoped to correct and adjust these ideas which at the time were a chaos swirling around in my hazy mind.—And I enjoyed this existence; I had no other; all my other plans had failed, and I still believed that I was better than the common masses. With great enthusiasm for anything that was called a mystery, I believed that what was most incomprehensible was also nearly always most venerable. I never joined the Rosicrucian Order (I believed the German Rosicrucians were inauthentic and ignorant), but greatly valued this ancient brotherhood after Schroeder's confidential revelation. Naturally, the notion of priesthood had become one of my favorite concepts, and if at that time someone would have requested I that I become a Jesuit, in a manner that would have flattered my understanding, he would not have met with much resistance. –

If anyone, who has played a similar role, or still plays it, would place his hand on his part and confess this as candidly as I, instead of turning up his nose at me or shrugging his shoulders in pity, then I believe truth and honesty could prevail. The reasonable and honest man, whose opinions and actions shape others, creates more harm by his silent agreement than an easily discovered fraud, who publicly cries out the system of nonsense.

But this disposition was increased in my mind all the more by harsh mental anguish and truly (if one may take my youth and inexperience into account) for the most part innocently incurred blows of fate, which made my heart extremely soft, wistful, receptive for sweet, religious melancholy, and so I tended to reach for anything that could elevate me above this world on the wings of philanthropic fantasies. Against these gentler emotions, however, struggled my natural activity, an unquiet spirit, spiritedness, carelessness, the recurrent pleasure that comes with influencing and working with all kinds of people, vanity and ambition—He who can combine all this in a single painting will be able to explain through it many contradictions in my actions and principles at that time. One such brave sample is a little piece I wrote at that time, giving it the grandiloquent title: *A General System for the People, etc.*[iii] It is full of pretentions and platitudes, a hodgepodge of healthy, bright reason and nonsense, Deism, and fantasy. A small, little-known book dealer accepted the manuscript on my request and printed the wretched thing; but to my greatest dismay, the only stir it created was that another, possibly just as crooked, head vehemently scolded it in Frankfurt's academic journal– a place worthy of the author, publisher, printer and reviewer; I thought this man did not know any better.

This is how it was when through the manuscript *The Bone of Contention*[iv] the entire honorable public was suddenly educated about the Strict Observance's Templar System. That was indeed a heavy blow for some men whose entire civic existence rested on this Templar Order, who had no other sphere of activity; for those, who as brothers in the order held the confidence of princes and commanded a certain degree of respect within Freemasonry for which they had also labored very hard through their personal efforts in a free association; finally for those who, based on the political and mystical expectations, fostered by the *quasi* Order of Templars, harbored hopes of power, wealth, honor and luster. Meanwhile, it was seriously contemplated how to heal the wound a perjurious traitor had opened. Arrangements were made for a general convention: and all zealous brothers were encouraged to present the superiors with suggestions for a beneficial establishment of the system and returning Freemasonry to a certain purpose. This also stirred in me the desire to do so.

I looked at the great host of Freemasons – men from all walks of life, among them so many noble, wise, active, powerful, wealthy men united by an *esprit de corps*, who did not know to what purpose; divided among themselves, unable to agree on opinions, without knowing who was groping in the dark the furthest, and this prevented them from working together for the benefit of humankind—what would they be able to achieve, had they been able to distinguish between speculations and actions, leaving some to the opinions of every single member, but directing others, according to certain principles, to work for the benefit of humanity and their brothers in particular, directing them according to laws that would make them faithfully stand by each other's side to pluck true merit from the dust, promote goodness and greatness through their secret influence, have every member work for the benefit of the state according to the measure of his abilities, since a closer brotherliness would give them the opportunity to better know people from all classes and rule them without hateful compulsion. Such ideas were familiar to us, and I preoccupied myself with them. According to these, I designed a plan suggesting means to combine all systems in certain main points, to assign each degree of the order a certain, effective sphere of activity, to use the coffers for great purposes through wise and honest management, and finally establish a separate class of researchers for the subject of mysticism, whose work, principles, and opinions would otherwise have no effect on the influence and activities of the order. I submitted my plan; it was read; I received polite letters regarding it; my assistance was requested for the upcoming convention; however, I soon believed to see, just how little the philanthropic, loving and unselfish intentions of the serene protectors and chiefs of Freemasonry through true and pure zeal and wise deliberation (indeed, how much work is required, what subtle methods, based on a deep study of man, to create a lasting, great work suitable for so many diverse people) were supported by the brothers of the order; how private interests enmeshed themselves and spurred sectarianism; how some people by secret machinations sought to use the entire convention to promote the sinister views of certain secret societies, and how it would be impossible to gather all these minds into a single fold—in short, I despaired at the thought of being able to accomplish anything useful at this convention. That, incidentally, I was convinced of the noble intentions of the superiors as well as some members of the Strict Observance even then; that I never doubted their goodwill, but very much the steadfastness of their principles, and the correctness of their understanding of what was necessary, useful and possible to do for the entire matter; and finally that I, free from attachment to any particular system, only wished the best for the order and the world is evidenced not only in the *Original Writings*, in which I attempt to convince the Illuminati from abandoning their prejudices against the Strict Observance, pointing out that they may be guilty of many inconsistencies, but not of outright fraud; but in this case, I refer to my preamble and commentaries of two volumes by Herr Beyerle, which I translated, namely *Oratio de conventu latomorum* and *Essay sur la Franc – Maçonnerie*[v], where I wholeheartedly agree, although I often feel that Herr Beyerle is unjust in his accusations, e.g. in his remarks on pages 77, 78, and 83 of the first volume, as well as in many other passages. However, my pamphlet *Contribution Toward the Latest History of Freemasons, in Nine Conversations*[vi], discusses this, primarily on pages 72-77.

While I thus discussed my intentions and concerns with various Freemasons, I made the acquaintance of Diomedes in July, 1780, who had been dispatched by the Illuminati in Bavaria to establish

Provinces in the Protestant colonies of this society wherever that was possible. I came to know him as a gracious man with a kind temperament and full of warmth for all that was good and noble; he visited me, and I often saw him in the company of three very honorable Freemasons, who were my friends, and also discussed with him my desires for a complete reformation of the order, adding, "Since I foresee that nothing useful or lasting will come of this convention, I am resolved to develop a new system with a circle of trusted, good brothers, scattered throughout Germany."

After I had finally revealed my views on this matter to him, he told me at once, "Why waste your efforts trying to create something new, when there is a society that has already accomplished what you seek and which is able to satisfy your thirst for knowledge and your eagerness to be active and useful; a society that is powerful and educated enough to do and teach everything you demand?"

One can imagine that my eyes grew wide when Diomedes (Marquis de C.) revealed this to me—me, who had cast his net so wide and so carefully in all my secret connections and all the branches of Masonry! This greatest, most important, and most perfect of all connections had remained hidden from me, and I had learned nothing of the fruits of their exalted labors?—My doubts were founded on this, but there was an answer to them, which would shut my mouth, "It is in this secret nature, where this society's greatest strength can be found; the unbroken preservation of the secret proves that the organization consists of solid, faithful persons, and as far as their operations are concerned, there are many things that occur in the world, whose outer effects are visible, but not their mainsprings." And so forth—This and a nod to the much publicized, almost miraculous progress of the Enlightenment in the imperial states, which hardly could have come to pass without the use of secret counsels, fully convinced me. I petitioned for membership, signed the revers, received the documents of the Minerval degree, was given an address of the honorable Celsus in Munich, and Diomedes continued departed.

In addition to myself, the Marquis in Frankfurt on the Main had also recruited the three above mentioned dear and good men, and we now worked together. I must confess that we, old Freemasons and certainly more than a little infected by the desire for mystery, and lusting after the secrets of the Freemason-Hieroglyphs, found the documents of the seed-school somewhat meager. A type of educational institution, operations for the basic education of younger persons, recommendations of books, which were already commonly known even among the lowest classes in the Protestant states – all these may have been well and necessary in the dark, Catholic Provinces, but our regions seemed to be too advanced for such a basic curriculum.

But there was a reasonable explanation for all this, namely, "The order has its eye primarily on young persons; it seeks to work for the benefit of the next generation. It can advance its cause better with uneducated persons than with ill-educated ones, and at this time nearly all adult persons have become depraved, even by their basic education, are full of demands, and are unable to be tuned to a single pitch. The order most certainly is headquartered in catholic states, but to operate in unison, it is not possible to adjust the lower grades to the requirements of each individual Province."—This made sense. We also noticed that the good people in Munich, with whom we corresponded, wrote in a terribly barbaric style, that even the papers of the Minerval-Degree were composed very poorly and incorrectly, and that in all matters, a despotic, commanding tone was employed, to which we, as free men, were not at all accustomed, and this could not be justified by the authority of the persons who spoke in this manner. However, this could be written off to the Catholic education system (for one may well think bright and profound thoughts, and still write poorly), and this seemed to be rooted in a solid conviction of the matter's intrinsic goodness and dignity. We merely insisted in not being treated as boys: we would no longer work for the cause, nor recruit new members, until we would be given deeper insight into the system. But this fell on deaf ears. My three fellow disciples, who had to attend certain business affairs, did not have the leisure to do school exercises and write their monthly *quibus licet* notes, and consequently, they withdrew; but I pursued the matter for a while, since I finally received a letter from Spartacus (Herr Weishaupt) in Ingolstadt in November 1780, in which he stated, "Upon the command of the superiors, I am continuing my correspondence with you. Discontinue your correspondence with Munich and keep the contents of your letters secret from any person."

These letters certainly were written in an entirely different spirit than those from Munich. Everything he said – and the manner in which he said it – did not fail to hit its mark, to inflame me for the cause of the order. Without sending me any further documents, he described a general picture "of a society, which by the finest and most secure means achieves the goal, to ensure the victory of virtue and wisdom over folly in the world, to achieve the most important discoveries in all areas of science, to mold its members into noble and great persons, and to ensure certain rewards even in this world for their perfection, to protect them from persecution, ill fate, and oppression, and tie the hands of any kind of despotism."

And as far as the means for achieving these exalted goals was concerned, he sent me several masterfully written elaborations with a request for my views on these documents, and this prompted the question, "What are the means by which human beings can be permanently united toward a great and good purpose without the use of external force?"

When at last even these proposed methods appeared to me brilliantly reasoned out and infallible, Herr Weishaupt explained these are the very methods employed by the order.

He promised me, "A new Heaven and a new Earth, a system that elevates humankind and the world, not quite to its height, but speeding toward it with firm steps, an alliance of the noblest, a holy legion of invincible warriors for wisdom and virtue."

Since he also noticed in me a desire for the higher sciences and speculative philosophy, he proceeded to promise me perfect satisfaction in this respect, as well. To prove this, he demonstrated to me his knowledge of ideas of diverse old and new philosophical sects, presented me with fragments of many a system for my evaluation, which formed the basis of his later curriculum about materialism and idealism, but without explaining which of these was the system of the order.

However, once he wrote me these very profound words regarding his certainty of the immortality of the soul, "It is this very aspect to which the order ascribes its tranquility. A short while ago, I lost my wife, whom I loved very much, to death, but I know for certain that I have not lost her for all eternity."

But he asked me not so much to think about these things, but rather about how to work most efficiently for the order, promising everything else as the wages for my labor, adding to this, "You can hold me to account, if not everything I promise comes true; I vouch for this with my honor."

Was anything more natural that to be inflamed by these letters, considering my disposition and my unusual spiritedness? To test my devotion, and before he could communicate the degrees above the Minerval-Class, he demanded that I first establish assemblies of this seed school and recruit more members. I did this eagerly, but I did request permission that, in the five large cities in the five German counties under my care, only to accept adult men who could bring the Great Work into operation. He approved this enthusiastically[14], and since I already had my eye on the best men in every Freemasonic system known to me, since I had planned to present them with my design for reforming Freemasonry, I invited them all to partake in the connection with the Illuminati, and in a short time, I had recruited a large number of noble, well-bred, learned, and important men as Minervals – men, whose names I only need to mention to prove it could not have been my intention to work a piece of knavery, men of whom could be expected that they would not allow themselves to be misused, nor led astray, and whom I most certainly would not have dared to entangle in a dangerous plan, even if Spartacus or I had harbored such dishonorable intentions. Herr

---

[14] See the postscript to the *Original Writings*, bottom of page 24.

Weishaupt was delighted with my good progress[15] and approved of my choices. Considering the state of Freemasonry at the time and the very low hopes of having accomplished anything great at the convention, all these men eagerly sought this connection which I described in such a favorable manner. I revealed to all these men the spirit Spartacus had breathed into me; supported by his word of honor, I gave my own for the greatness and goodness of the cause. Where he wrote warmly of the order, I wrote about it with the greatest enthusiasm. Where he promised Elysium, I, true to my temper, promised Paradise. However, I soon realized that my enthusiasm in this had gone too far, and I began to be more careful with my promises. The imaginations of the new members alone painted the picture I had laid before them in their own colors. Every man in the order believed to find what he had been searching for, and what he promised himself, he ultimately believed I had promised, and it was my duty to deliver on these promises. Everyone recruited his best friends, and the matter developed with unimaginable speed. I could no longer stem this tide and no longer oversee the smaller details. Many who were not suitable were accepted after

---

[15] Postscript to the *Original Writings*, bottom of page 28 and bottom of page 69

repeated and urgent requests; soon, I was dealing with several hundred people, all of whom demanded that I satisfy and teach them, who sought the fulfillment of their heart's desire through me, and day and night, I had to offer up all my physical, economical and intellectual resources in order to avoid moral bankruptcy. Everyone wanted to receive, but no one wanted to give; no one could place himself in my frightful position, toilsome beyond words. If a forester wanted to know, what types of wood grew best in this soil or that, he enquired with the order. If a chemist wanted to know, which kind of phosphorous was best to manufacture, the order was expected to provide him with that information. Many demanded promotions to services and positions of honor; others monetary advances, prepayments for books they intended to write and use the order to trumpet them out; others requested considerable loans to become debt-free. Others requested that the order negotiate marriages or arrangements or solicit legal proceedings on their behalf. And when I sought help from this supposedly existing higher order, Spartacus answered repeatedly that each Province had to care for its own people, and so everything fell back on me, who was only one person. And since I did not possess any higher degrees, I could not install any subordinate leaders who could have shouldered part of this burden, because I was not in a position to properly instruct them. And how easily they became discouraged—yes! impolite and defiant, regardless of the fact I hadn't taken a penny from anyone, if I did not satisfy their every desire. So I did what was humanly possible, and thus I discovered what a man can accomplish when his zeal and activity are stretched to the limit. I well knew that in order to properly reply to a *quibus licet*, I sometimes had to write to ten other people; but it sufficed, and everyone was satisfied, and everyone believed in the order's omnipotence. My garden house near Frankfurt on the Main became an office in which mutual services were concentrated. All the while, I led a simple, anonymous life (apart from frequent visits by traveling members of the order), lived outside all networks with princes and their courts – a place which, thanks to the much too outspoken tone of my writings I had at least not then occupied; without help, without assistance I gave out by frequent exchanges of services among its members which I set in motion through my wide ranging correspondence, without them knowing at times for whom they were working, honors, sinecures, dignities and in the name of the nonexistent superiors, I gave fortune's approbation to those I considered most worthy. Quite often, family counsels and professional secrets were placed in my lap—so deep was these people's trust in my person, because we always went about our work with them so unselfishly and honestly[16]. A large part of these things was seen only by my eyes and I can recall having been guilty of only a single well-intentioned indiscretion on my part, which was of no consequence to me, however, other than that Herr von B***, whom it concerned, misjudged me in the matter. It should be noted, by the way, that I am not singing my own praises with all this, because my only merit lies within my activities; the cause itself accomplished the great effects. Spartacus and I were equally innocent of many good and evil things that followed thereafter—a plan was made; ah! and as so soften, the result differed greatly from what we had imagined!

Although there were nearly always several younger Brothers in my room who were busy with copying, and I also employed two sworn copyists, the essentials and the more important correspondence had to be performed by me. My health deteriorated markedly, and my purse was strained

---

[16] Refer to what Herr Weishaupt has to say about this in the postscript to the *Original Writings*, middle of page 46.

from postage expenses and the short trips (I was reimbursed for a few longer trips by those, on whose behalf I traveled); for a while, I even had to pawn what little silverware I possessed. I admit it would have been an easy task to achieve material gain through the connections with great men, which I made with my correspondences. Indeed! I, and as far as I know, Herr Weishaupt, were approached with sometimes very enticing offers of the kind, which we, however, honorably turned down.

When I thus realized the order's power to do good grew with each day, and I was furthermore convinced that Spartacus and I most certainly had the purest intentions in all these things, I could not close my eyes to the possibility that this machine, in the hands of scheming, ambitious, and power hungry persons (and these could have sooner or later pushed their way up in the order and placed themselves at the system's head) could become a great danger to humankind. Therefore my driving thought was to prevent this, wherever possible, as will be seen hereafter.

At the time, the Jesuits and the German Rosicrucians seemed equally dangerous to the order and the rest of the world. Therefore, documents were sent to me as evidence against the former, and I included them in my correspondence to Schloetzer, and after I received more detailed news and I read Chalotais'[vii] work and other selected news, I wrote the pamphlet *About Jesuits, Freemasons and German Rosicrucians[viii]*—certain ly only out of zeal for the good cause of reason and liberty, because at the time, I had never knowingly spoken with a Jesuit, and I have never had anything to do with the German Rosicrucians for good or ill.

Then, Spartacus was so satisfied with me that his letters were filled with enthusiastic praise for my efforts.

"Your service against the Jesuits," he wrote. "I shall not forget as long as there is breath in my body.—With six of Philo's caliber I would dare to reform the entire world.—Only few men like Philo are born every few thousand years.—Let Philo school you[17] "—and more of such well-meaning flatteries that tickled my vanity and stirred my zeal.

In that time, Herr Weishaupt sent me a part of his lesser Illuminatus-Degree, his masterpiece indeed, which was so well-liked by the best of my members

---

[17] *Original Writings*, bottom of page 363

and which inflamed them so much, that for a while, they sought no further advancement in the order.

Of course, here and there we had our share of troublesome incidents. When I objected or didn't object to the selection of a new member, supported by one and opposed by another, I fell out of favor with one party on several occasions. When persons violated the law of secrecy and two people, who were prejudiced against one another or even were enemies, through gossip learned that they belonged to the same order, one of them usually wanted to resign or at least confronted me about this. But I did not owe them an explanation, and herein lay the greatness of the order: that persons, who in their civic life would not have tolerated each other in a common endeavor, were pulling on the same rope without knowing this, working together for a common good, and perhaps were even performing services for each other, because everything was managed by third parties. If someone unbidden and against my orders traveled to new cities for recruitment purposes, and the person working for the order in that place learned of it, that person became my enemy. When a restless spirit in the order was not immediately satisfied in his curiosity, found himself corrected in his favorite opinion, or the slightest hint of mistrust arose in him, such a man thought I was a windbag on one occasion, a fraud on another, and a secret Jesuit on still another. I had to wear many different hats[18], depending on the people's dispositions, to make the order interesting to them, which certainly would have made a poor impression of my character at length. Had one heard the various opinions of me at that time, one would have learned that while I was considered a staunch freethinker and deist in one region, I was a religious dreamer in another, that I was described as a tireless, shrewd negotiator in one place, and a speculating breeder of secrets in another. I often had to hide my true beliefs, had to use the language of each man to unite so many different minds and bring them closer to one another. It is from this perspective, if one is to judge equitably, that many remarks in my letters, which can be found in the *Original Writings* must be viewed. In Catholic states, nearly all members had the same desire, which was the fall of religious despotism, but in the protestant regions, things looked very different. Of all people, Herr Weishaupt was the least able to put himself in my position; he who generally wasn't directly

---

[18] Postscript to the *Original Writings,* middle of page 101

concerned with the members' training and dispositions, but sat among his books and made new plans, making use of our experiences to perfect the system, but was not always fair-minded enough to convince himself that I had to purchase these experiences often at the expense of incurring damages, but without blame.

The Minerval-Class did not progress at all in the Protestant states, and indeed, this institution was generally useful only in the dark, Catholic Provinces and for mediocre everyday people. However, Herr Weishaupt did not deign to see it this way. He unceasingly insisted on holding these assemblies, and even then, he assigned me a certain portion of the blame when my attempts failed with a few individuals, albeit only in the most polite terms.

But the less the members were inclined to attend the classes of the seed school, the more eagerly they urged me to finally communicate the higher degrees to them. The many deceits, which had been committed in Freemasonry, had made everyone mistrustful of secret leaders and put everyone on guard. They feared that, in the end, underneath this best of all facades was a building full of treacherous blind alleys, although they did not let it show. In part, they also yearned for the explanation of the Masonic glyphs, all sorts of secrets, and presented many questions to the superiors, that I was unable to answer, since I myself did not know the order's principles regarding certain things. In addition, I no longer was able to preside over the entire work; to prevent the whole matter form falling into confusion, I needed to institute subordinates, and in order for them to be of any use, they needed to be instructed in the entire system. I therefore at last, seriously urged for the entire presentation of the system, referring to my hitherto tireless zeal, to prove that I was not unworthy of their unrestricted trust.

And now, Spartacus at last revealed his great secret.

"The order does not yet exist, only in my mind. Only the lower class, the seed school has been established in a few Catholic Provinces; but I have assembled the most magnificent materials en masse for the higher degrees. Would you," he wrote. "Forgive my little fraud? I have long yearned to find worthy collaborators for this great work, but have found none, other than you, who penetrate into the spirit of the system as deeply as I do and is so conscientiously and tirelessly active. You, then, are the man whom Heaven has brought into my life for my happiness. I place myself entirely into your hands. I will send you all my documents. You shall develop the whole thing, modify it according to your judgment, and entrust the history of the foundation with as many of your members as you deem necessary, to ease your burden and to assist me as counsels. I no longer wish to be chief, but be your subordinate. However, so we can discuss all these things in person, and so you can ascertain what kind of people you are working with, I ask that you travel to Bavaria. The brothers, who yearn to see you from the bottom of their hearts, are willing to reimburse your travel expenses."

Such a revelation placed me in an unprecedented dilemma. How was I to satisfy all these men, in whom I had raised the highest hopes, to whom I had given my word of honor about the magnitude and importance of the matter? What was I to do?—To publicly expose a man, whose truly honorable intentions could not be denied, but who had acted so inconsistently? Of course I could have simply withdrawn from all this, but at the same time, the whole edifice would have collapsed – and how could I wish for that when I saw the most magnificent fruits of my labors everywhere, and I could rightfully hope, that, once those higher degrees were established, I could keep the promises I had made my people?

Thus I wrote to Spartacus, "I am resolved not to desert you. The lust for secrets has never been my main motivation, but the desire to be active and useful on behalf of what is good, has always been the end of my desires. I see the best opportunity for this here, and therefore I am indifferent as to whether the order is old or new or merely a project. To the contrary, the latter is closer to my desires, because now everything can be better tailored toward the Protestant regions and the connection to the Freemasons. I find this consideration all the more important, since so many persons feel so strongly about it, are already united in the cause through their *esprit the corps*, expected so much of the Masonic hieroglyphs, that this sentiment, to explain the symbols according to our system and at last guide all of Freemasonry toward our exalted purpose and bring it under guidance, cannot be ignored. At this time, I am not yet inclined to share the foundation history with several members or establish so-called Areopagites. But at any rate, it is of the utmost importance to complete the higher degrees as quickly as possible and to install superiors in all locations. And by the way, I am willing to meet in person."

Thus in November 1781, I traveled through Swabia and Franconia to Bavaria, getting to know personally the largest number of the members of the order not under my direction, was received and cared for by them with such excellent veneration, faithfulness, and tenderness, nursed so well during a small illness in Eichstadt, that the memory of it and my brotherly love toward many a noble man will never depart from my soul. Thus I shall never forget the hours I spent within the circle of my dear friend Celsus' honorable family, where he, his honest and judicious wife, and his loveable daughter treated me like their son and brother. My heart is moved to joy when I think of the house of the excellent Alfred and his worthy spouse, of Arrian's kindness, Hannibal's honest hospitality, of Scaliger's diligence, of my mirthful stay in Freisingen, of the gentle Alcibiades – in short! I have fond memories of nearly all brothers with whom I stayed.

However, as I render my public testimony of my high regard for so many brave men, I must not keep silent of what displeased me, and in what condition I found the order in these regions.

Spartacus was undoubtedly a brilliant mind, a profound thinker, all the more deserving of respect and admiration, since he had to obtain his education in the midst of a mindless Catholic educational system, so his brilliance can be credited only to his own reasoning and his reading of good books, which in these regions can only be obtained under considerable difficulties that deter many people. At the same time his heart was ablaze with an unmatched selfless zeal to accomplish something great and useful for humanity, and few difficulties deterred him. But I also noticed in him a trait, which later I so often recognized as the mark of a great genius: small obstacles and bantering discouraged him and made him feel uncomfortable; greater misfortunes, on the other hand brought out, as he later demonstrated, his entire steadfastness, allowing him to concentrate all his strength to shoulder great burdens and resist adversity. The other side of the coin was that he had no practical knowledge of human nature at the time. He had gleaned most of his ideas concerning what good can be done in the world from books, in which he, with his keen intellect, certainly understood how to separate truth and wisdom from prejudice, declamation, and weakness. Still, he could not refrain, no matter how correct his thoughts, to embellish his letters with the s.p.d.[ix], the mottos, and the unbearably numerous citations from old and new books in such a pedantic manner, that these empty phrases, this professorial tone, weakened his expressiveness, of what was otherwise was his heartfelt eloquence.—Later, he also made great progress in this aspect. Since furthermore, his practical study of human nature had been limited to his extensive knowledge of the Jesuit order's constitution and the manner in which these fathers conducted themselves toward their children, his governing idea was to use those means for good, which that order used for evil purposes. This was his most cherished idea – an idea whose impossibility one must soon notice as soon as one begins with the work. However, this led to the fact, that he did not always think ill of his choice of tools he intended to use for good purposes[19]. He was therefore convinced, that a despotism of the leaders against the subordinates, whose blind obedience he demanded, was necessary, but without the coercive means freely available to the Jesuits, which we did not have and which were not practicable in a free, not publicly sanctioned society. This explains[20] why he pressed

---

[19] One should not forget that I am speaking of Herr W.'s then held beliefs, which were later corrected through better experiences and reflection.
[20] Refer to Spartacus' letters to Cato in the *Original Writings*

for the limitless force of a general, to remove us confidants, to separate us from one another, prevent subsequent conventions[21] and explications, not to share all regional news with the Corps of Areopagites, and to never admit that any man was indispensable, even if the whole matter would collapse over this. This certainly would have occurred, and his order would have eternally remained a chimera, had fortune not delivered unto him so many active members. All the while he did not really do anything as far as the execution of his plan was concerned, and even this plan only matured by and by through our practical experiences, which he quietly and with cool reasoning could compare and utilize for the perfection of his system. By the way, Spartacus enjoyed among his impartial fellow citizens a reputation of scholarliness, wisdom, and impeccable morality. He led a moderate, respectable life, and completed his business affairs faithfully.—Such was the man's character, whose courage, zeal and noble, good will is certainly deserving of admiration. At the very least, he should be given credit for having wakened many a sleeping power through the founding of his order, regardless of how weak and insignificant it may

---

[21] *Original Writings*, top of page 385

have been at first, having caused many good effects, enriching the history of humankind and the science of psychology!—Now we shall talk about his first collaborators!

We heard that in the beginning that Herr Weishaupt's plan was only to raise young people in the spirit of the order, not to count on the fruits of his labor during his lifetime, but to place the thus educated youths at the highest place of his work that they may then educate the next generation. This principle certainly was noble and unselfish, but it was just as impossible to execute. Permit me to elaborate this point a little! I have already discussed in passing the impossibility of using Jesuit methods for good purposes without this sooner or later spiraling out of control and becoming subject to abuse. On other occasions, I have discussed this more broadly[22x]. Let us now investigate the difficulties one must encounter, which struck Herr Weishaupt in full measure, when one seeks to educate one's own collaborators.

---

[22] Refer to *The Errors of the Philosopher, or the Story of Ludwig of Seelberg*, Pt. 2, Chap. 11, 12 and 13. And *On Human Relations,* Part 2, Chap. 8. And *The History of Peter Clausen*, Part 2, pages 157 through 166. These passages contain my experience-based beliefs about such secret societies; however, I wish from the bottom of my heart, someone would disprove me in theory and in practice.

It could not be expected of young persons to become highly enthused about being benefactors for the human race. Thus, in order to instill in them this enthusiasm, they needed to be educated with careful diligence. Had a man succeeded in this endeavor with two youths, and these youths had in turn educated in turn two more, a whole century would have passed, before it could be said an order had been founded. These few people would have basically done nothing more than any other wise house father: to raise a few children according to his best ability to become good, wise, and charitable human beings. But if this plan was to be implemented for a true order, one had to begin with a larger number of young people. But in the absence of external coercion and all public sanction, it was necessary to devise motivations to attract young people to place themselves under the protection of those who on their own decided to become their educators. These motivations had to be drawn from the interests of each of individual. Subsequently, one had to be able to promise them external, guaranteed advantages, and such a promise required power, required that what was to be founded, was already in existence. If one were working with a larger number of younger persons, one could neither observe them sufficiently nor educate them properly. One therefore needed adult co-workers, and since these were not inclined to let themselves be reeducated, the first idea, to use self-created tools, certainly was lost. However, I considered the latter path more feasible: to begin by choosing a sufficient number of solid, educated men as colleagues and to begin by working from the top down. Indeed, every man brought with him his own opinions, which he was eager to voice; thus, the entire order could not be formed according to the ideal of a single man, governed absolutely at the nod of a single man who was accountable to no one. Men wanted to think for themselves, rather than be led blindly. But through this process, a varied mixture of manly ideas could enter into the whole matter. Six good heads can see further than one good head, or a man would have to believe, he was the only man on God's green earth who had a sense of what was good and profitable for the human race. This would also make it more difficult for the highest power to be abused or that despotism could creep in – in short, I would have always considered it more advisable to make the initial arrangements with a few wise and secure men and then begin with the execution. But unfortunately, Herr Weishaupt lived in such circumstances that made it difficult for him to find a number of such men. Furthermore, this would not have been in accordance with his system. Thus, he had no other choice than to choose from among his young students those he could hope to wholly educate according to his plan, to completely fill them with his spirit. One can hear from himself, whether or not he had any luck in this. In the *Postscript to the Original Writings*, page 39, he characterizes them as having a little too much of that crude Bavarian naiveté.

"Socrates," he said. "who is a capital man, is always drunk. Augustus has a most terrible reputation, and Alcibiades sits with the serving wench all day and sighs and suffers. Tiberius sought to violate Decomedes' sister in Corinth, and the man accomplished this. For Heaven's sake, what kind of Areopagites are these?"

And in the first collection of the *Original Writings*, page 367, he writes of the deplorable condition of the order in the Province of Bavaria,

"If Philo learned of all these things, he would immediately resign, he who believes to have found only order, beauty and the most excellent edifice even after his discovery. Not only Your Province, but all which are under the direction of the Athenian Areopagites (his first and most noble co-workers) are in a state of utter wretchedness."

Far be it from me to reprimand this so I can level a bitter accusation against Herr Weishaupt; I cite it only in my own defense. For Spartacus does complain to Cato[23] in his letters about my own lack of care in the recruiting and examination of the members. However, if one considers what an unbelievable complex machine I had to supervise and how unfortunate the founder himself had been in the selection and education of his initial few colleagues, I believe that one must, instead of accusing me of rashness in my actions, one should rather deplore the imperfection of all earthly endeavors, the weakness of the human spirit – even when the heart is in the right place – and the most faithful efforts. But at least I can make the bold claim that of all those whom I brought to the order, even by third or fourth hand, there was not one, to whom a single characteristic with which Spartacus described his own Areopagites, applies. I do not know, if these descriptions were exaggerated or not; but what I do know is that a quite a few of the Areopagites and the members, whom I got to know on my journey were very lovable, brave men, as I have already said. Celsus and Cato and others who served were not among the original founders, but entered the order at a

---

[23] *Original Writings*, page 384 and *Postscript*, page 69

later point; however, even among those first Areopagites were noble people, who lacked neither in mental faculty nor righteousness of the heart. But I confess that I did not meet a single one of whom I thought he had the calling to stand at the helm of such a great and important work, not to mention found such an endeavor. Among them, only Cato actively worked for the order. The others did not take the quill in hand. They were too distracted and too preoccupied with the pursuit of pleasure[24], at times overwhelmed with business matters; and still they did not want that anything happened without them. No one had much knowledge of the world, any kind of refined, practical knowledge of anthropology, experience with secret societies, knowledge of the Masonic system, and Spartacus had next to no knowledge at all. The question what the order's ultimate purpose should be was still raised among them. Promoting the public's enlightenment, protecting and supporting one another, and elevating every member in his civic life according to his merit and ability – that certainly was the governing idea among all. However their understanding regarding this enlightenment was very vague. In wholly Catholic states, with their shoddy education of the

---

[24] *Postscript of the Original Writings*, bottom of page 39

youth and their impracticable curriculum in religious matters, it is not an unusual phenomenon that people who have thus been educated, throw out the baby with the bath water and toss all positive religion onto the ash heap, when they open their eyes and want to break the chains of superstition. However, for men who seek to establish a system for the welfare of the world, these principles are not the wisest: I found that they spoke with entirely too little restraint about religion, faith and revelation – by the way, I gladly leave it to every person to care for the peace of his soul in his own manner – that they were intolerant against good people whom they could accuse of nothing more that they adhered to a religious doctrine and were not ready to dismiss these teachings until they could receive something more reassuring and more proven in their place. I had to tune myself to this melody somewhat to win their trust, as can also be seen in the *Original Writings* and as will be seen later, this led me to the idea of incorporating a sort of explanation of the Christian religious teachings and practices into the system that would satisfy all parties (Spartacus had arrived at the same idea simultaneously). As far as the purity of their morals was concerned, there is much to be remembered from this aspect, as well. Far be it from me to judge the actions of others.

Who knows what struggles between principles and passions even the wisest and best man has to fight every hour? And I may have more than one cause to be tolerant so that I may deserve the same sufferance and forgiveness. Neither do I wish to claim that liberal principles in matters of religion should be equated with poor morality. However, it cannot be denied that one is entitled to demand of men who take up the cause of reforming and enlightening the most sacred matters, that by their example and transformation they prove the goodness and usefulness of their teaching, even if only as to not show weakness before the enemies of truth, who would cite them as the pitfalls of true enlightenment. I further did not like the way in which they meddled in political matters and procured civil advantages to the members of the order. But in their defense, one may assume that the enemies of the good cause were active in these areas and had a tremendous influence in government affairs, as I was assured, using such measures, that could almost justify the use of similar countermeasures. On the other hand it would not be just to hold the entire order, even in the state in which it was at the time, accountable for some passages of the kind as are found in the *Original Writings* which in part were mere opinions, suggestions, or brash endeavors of fiery, carless youths. The Areopagite Ajax was indeed one of those whole believed that sometimes dishonorable ways seemed permissible, but these steps were not approved by the others, and yes! they ultimately completely separated themselves from him before I arrived in Bavaria. I must also remind the reader that I do not know this young man in the least, but only know what others have told me about him.

In addition to these not altogether desirable circumstances came the fact that all the Areopagites were thoroughly fed up with Spartacus. Even before I came to Munich, their letters had not painted a very flattering picture of him[25]. They complained about his obstinacy, his despotism, the Jesuit manner in which he kept them separate so he could rule them by this division, his inconsistency regarding his principles, the mutability of his affections, and the uncertainty of his trust.

They complained, "He requires that others do everything, while he has basically done nothing but to make plans he himself is unable to execute. He believes himself to be chief of all men, a Messiah, and treats no one with justice, only those

---

[25] *Postscript to the Original Writings,* top of page 80

for flatter him. Such a man he elevates to the Heavens for a while. However, a minor circumstance, a lack of blind devotion to his whims, can lower the noblest man in his esteem, while on the other hand, a little a little cow-towing and homage will assure even the most crooked head his unlimited trust."

To this, they added, "His heart knows neither gratitude nor concern for a person's well-being. He loves and uses people only as long as he finds their ideas useful, and you will fare no better."

I saw in these descriptions more bitterness than truth. Indeed, I could not fully absolve Spartacus from despotism, obstinacy, and pride; however, these flaws were rooted his conviction that such an engine indeed needed to be operated by a single head. His obstinacy and pride, on the other hand, rested on his intrinsic belief in his own worth[26]. In the meantime, I had a yet another obstacle to overcome, to make peace among the brothers, without whom nothing could be done, after all.

By the way, the most sincere goodwill and the most faithful zeal of all members shone through

---

[26] One can find such an example in the *Postscript to the Original Writings,* page 81.

these imperfections. Their hearts were aflame with the noblest intentions to do good and great things. They were dedicated to the order with the warmest faithfulness. They did not always choose the best means, but this was due to their lack of understanding. Their inactivity was not rooted in malice, and where the best of the whole matter was concerned, all of them were willing to forget their private quarrels.—This was the state of the order in Bavaria as I saw it!

Thus I commenced to reconcile the Areopagites with Spartacus, which did not require much effort[27] . Following this, I appeared as a delegate of the Secret High Chiefs, on the request of Weishaupt and the others, to increase the society's respectability there, attended a few assemblies, examined as an authorized *Visiteur* the state of the seed schools in the various areas, encouraged, inspired, decreed, consoled, won a few respected and noble men over to the order, acquainted the Areopagites with the various Masonic systems, and made oral and written agreements with my fellow members concerning our future operations.

The main points of this contract were:

---

[27] Refer to the introduction of the Baron of Bassus to the heads of state of the Republic of Grisons.

1. All materials concerning the higher degrees and essays by Spartacus were to be handed over to me, and it was left up to me to use as much of this material as I saw fit – even to modify the documents of the already established Minerval Class – as I was tasked to develop the entire system with respect to the greater mysteries, and then to submit my work to the Corps of Areopagites. Every one of these was to add his own comments. All this was to be submitted to Herr Weishaupt in the end, and when he had passed his final judgment, copied all degrees, and authenticated them, he was to introduce them to all regions. No changes were to be made to these until a subsequent convention of the Areopagites.

2. My suggestion to tie everything to Freemasonry was to be approved, indeed! from the lofty Illuminatus degree on, everything was to be rooted in and adjusted to Freemasonry. A Freemason Ritual for the three symbolic degrees and constitution book was to be developed, introduced to all lodges, as much as it was possible, and enacted through the influence of our members, so that our people would gain the upper hand in the lodges of the various systems and the idle houses of

Freemasonry could be activated for the good cause. I did all these things.

3. I was given a free hand to introduce myself to all those honest and articulate brothers at the Masonic Congress in Wilhelmsbad[xi] whom I deemed capable of appreciating the importance of such a system without selfishness, prejudice, and egotism and to replace empty dalliance and hieroglyphic games.

4. I was assured repeatedly that I was free to promote as many members to Areopagites and install all many chiefs as I deemed necessary and useful to assist me in my efforts.

5. I set the condition that no books attacking the teachings of the Christian religion would be recommended to the brothers I had accepted and who were subordinate to me, that caution needed to be exercised with regard to our obligations and relations with the states, and that in general, the entire religious and political principles up to the greater mysteries, which required the most mature deliberations, should be put off and not be developed at the time.

6. Since I still could not shake the fear, the order's eventual truly fearsome power could be abused by power hungry persons, and I also feared our own passions, if we founders – we, who could wield our power in the name of unknown chiefs

– could not keep ourselves in check. I proposed a kind of republican government. I thus urgently implored the chiefs that each of us select from among his subordinates the best and most able persons and to give them proper instructions which were to be compiled into a Regent Degree. To this Regent Class, the entire government of the order was to be surrendered. There were to fill from among themselves the highest offices, that is the Provincial Inspectors – indeed! the National Chief positions through election and agreement among one another. None of the Areopagites was to fill such an office, but we wanted to merely constitute a College of Chiefs, whose president was to be Spartacus. The National Chiefs' reports were to be sent to this college. We would control and supervise all Chiefs of the order, powerless to abuse our authority, since all the details would rest in the hands of the Regent Class. We furthermore obligated ourselves not to keep even the least, important news from one another.—I no longer possess any documents regarding this agreement, but I do know that my former brothers are too honest to deny its contents.

When this was altogether put in order[28], I traveled back to Frankfurt and proceeded to begin working on this task. I began by attempting to see, if could prepare those Brother Masons who wielded the most influence at the next Freemasonic Convention for the acceptance of such a system. I admit that I still cultivated a certain attachment to the Strict Observance, and since so many member of this order had become Illuminati through me, I thus flattered myself with the hope that both systems could be merged. But I certainly was neither inclined nor authorized by my brothers to present all documents to the entire Congress and to submit ourselves to the mercy or disfavor and surrender ourselves to a society, from which we (who demanded no power through social standing, nobility and wealth, but through unity and consistency in our plan) could basically expect no advantages and whose members were not united in a common cause, who were not trained in accordance to our purposes, who wanted to shine and rule publicly, while our entire constitution was based on operating quietly and in secrecy.

However, I say I made the attempt. I conducted my services orally and in writing, but in every case,

---

[28] Refer to the beginning of Hannibal's letters in the *Postscript to the Original Writings*, bottom of page 134.

I received the same, somewhat frustrating answer, "Please send me your documents or present them at the congress, and then we shall see what is useful and what is not."

In the full knowledge of our own strength, compared to the Strict Observance's weakness, disunity, its unsystematic character and its lack of a secure footing, and considering that it had recently proven that the foundation on which it had erected its building was shaky at best, and that it had consequently wholly relieved us of our obligations based thereon, I believed I had done more than enough. I gave up all hopes of coming to an agreement with the entire convention, and I was still resolved to convince and win over individual members and lodges and thereby to prevent that fantasy and fraudulence would not become more influential than we and that the Masonic Order would not fall under its control. To accomplish this, Minos was asked to maintain a watchful eye in Wilhelmsbad (I had surrendered my mandate as delegate, and I did not attend the congress in any official capacity). But I demonstrated in word and deed, that I was willing to accept each and every one of these honest and wise brothers attending who wished to visit me in Frankfurt, not merely to research, discover or peruse, but join us according to our institutions, inasmuch as we could deliver on the promises we made in the First Degree. Consequently, I enjoyed the satisfaction of seeing that, after the well-intentioned purposes for which these men had gathered from all corners of the Masonic world, did not bring about the desired results because no one could agree on the basic principles, several of these men became convinced that their desire to work toward the betterment of humanity could be better fulfilled by accepting our help and thus eagerly accepted our system. Incidentally how harmless my intentions at the Wilhelmsbad Congress were, is documented in my report of the event, which can be found in the *Postscript to the Original Writings,* page 209, ff.—Only a truly partisan mind would believe that it is dangerous and forbidden to endeavor the modification of a work one deems inefficient and useless, to say the least, without harboring the slightest selfish or private motivation.

In the meantime, I had also developed our entire system, and in order to understand what kind of work was involved here, I ask that I be permitted to summarize what considerations I had to make and what principles affected the matter. First of all, as far as I was concerned: I have already stated that my deeds and thoughts were influenced by a combination of a desire to be active, an inclination for mysticism and mild fantasy. It was to be expected that my efforts bore this stamp. As far as Spartacus was concerned, I had to use his essays as the basis of my work. It is well known what their general gist was, and that he mainly sought to imitate the Jesuit Order, but meant to use its institutions for good purposes. Further, the entire system had to be applicable to Freemasonry and its hieroglyphs—This presented another difficulty, which caused Herr Weishaupt to write this about me (*Postscript to the Original Writings*, top of page 67), "Leave out the gibberish, half-theosophical address of the Scottish Knight degrees composed by Philo and the explanation of the hieroglyphs!"

However, the completed degrees could not be changed in their main parts, because they had already been given to several hundred people! And finally, the heart of the matter! The entire system needed to be interesting for everyone and not objectionable in the least to anyone. However, among us (because we had all joined the order before we had a solid system) were confirmed Deists, religious dreamers, brooders, alchemists, theosophists, those who loved serenity and did not like to do much work, restless spirits, those who were inclined to intrigues, industrious and active persons, those who lusted for power, ambitious persons, those who prided themselves in their ancestry, selfish persons, those who sought advancement in their civic life, and others who sought help in academic projects, some who enjoyed celebrations and others who scorned anything that was called a ceremony, philosophers and philosophizers—in short! people from many backgrounds, dispositions, abilities and temperaments—I believe it is sufficient to say on behalf of the entire order and myself that the system, which needed to suit all these people as much as possible, may not present to everyone a picture of perfection.

And now I would like to present a sketch of this system. How much of this, as far as conceptualization and development is concerned, flowed out of my head and heart, how much on the other hand, belongs to Herr Weishaupt, and what at last, stems from the various Areopagites, that can at this point not be separated very easily. Some of those who have read these degrees may recognize the respective author from the style in individual passages; however, that is irrelevant—it must suffice that they are the true degrees of these

Illuminati of whom I was a member, and that nothing can be found in these that would be unworthy of an honorable man! I will also make do with merely rendering a sketch of the entire matter, as I have said, and I will refer the reader to those sources where he can read most of these degrees printed in detail.

The system of the Illuminati was divided into three main classes, each of which was divided into two subsections. First was the seed school, which included the Novitiate and the Minerval Class. Then followed Masonry, symbolic and Scottish, and finally, the Mysteries Class, which included the lesser and greater mysteries.

From the time that the order had more adult, educated persons than rough youths, it was no longer possible to blindly lead them, to treat them as pupils in a society whose main purpose was not even made known to them even in general, to demand from them obedience and an accounting of their progress in areas of knowledge they had already learned as boys, and to promise them protection and enlightenment in the sciences we could more likely expect from them. However, it was still necessary that they would not only be acquainted with the system of the seed school, but also to develop their principles and attune them to our purpose by presenting them with a number of questions they were expected to answer. I also had developed a preparatory essay, titled "A General Understanding of the Illuminati Society," which had actually been intended for more advanced candidates, but which generally was presented to all candidates and which included a general explanation of the order's main purposes and the excellent means used to attain them.

Then there was the Novitiate. Here, the pupil did not get to know his guide, who in turn strove to discover, if the young man would even be of use to us, if he was capable, receptive, obedient and loyal to the purpose made known to him. If he was not, he was abandoned; if, on the other hand, he showed promise, he was accepted into the Minerval Class. Here, he worked together with a few other Minervals under the supervision of the Minerval Magistrate, was required to report on his progress on a monthly basis and was obligated to deliver sealed notes to the magistrates in which he stated whether or not he was satisfied with his immediate superior, what he desired and what he could do or had done for the benefit of the society. He was promised and given support and elucidation in a certain literary subject in which he had enrolled, promised consequently adequate care in his civic life, according to his merit and progress, as well as protection against persecution and affronts. In return, he was obligated, when ordered by the chiefs, to gather information and perform research within his subject for the benefit of the whole, and to perform small tasks given to him without complaint.

Had he thus worked for a while, he would be accepted into some lodge that was already under our direction, or in which we through the influence of our people were in the process of achieving the majority. He had to attempt to attain the three symbolic degrees in order, and if he so pleased, several others as long as he paid for this himself. But with us, he remained in the previous connection, and if he did not demonstrate sufficient ability to further advance in our system, he now had an additional, wide field in which he could spend his leisure time deciphering the Masonic Glyphs and do some insignificant lodge work. But if he was cut from a better cloth, we promoted him to the lesser Illuminatus Degree when he became a Master Mason.

Here, he was given special supervision over a few pupils on whose progress he had to report in the minutest detail. He was instructed in how people had to be educated and governed. He received pointers allowing him to look more thoroughly into the system. This then, was the degree, mainly authored by Spartacus, which met with general applause and which could indeed be called his masterpiece. Where Minerval Assemblies were founded, four of such lesser Illuminati formed the Magistrates or their heads and directed the efforts of this class.

By occupying oneself with the study and education of others, one naturally gains knowledge about human beings and especially knowledge of oneself. However, it seemed important that this field of study be the work of its own degree, and this is what occurred in the greater Illuminatus degree, or Scottish Novitiate. Here, several thousand questions were raised by which the inner and outer character of man was to be researched. By comparing all these character traits, even the smallest and seemingly insignificant ones, the most wonderful general anthropological results could be obtained, and gradually a certain semiotic of the soul could be developed. Furthermore, the work of this degree was mostly to investigate in these assemblies the finer character nuances of the lesser Illuminati according to these questions. Each greater Illuminatus was to have a few lesser Illuminati under his secret supervision. No one was to be promoted to this degree until his supervisor had answered all these questions about the candidate. Thus, it would have been impossible that an unworthy person, someone whose slightest secret of the heart was unknown, could have forced his way to the peak of our system. A lack of workers certainly caused us to accept and promote many people with whom these operations could not be conducted. Only by henceforth observing strict adherence, we would be able to gradually separate the wheat from the chaff. The members of this degree were also obliged to report on a monthly basis: which services and benefits they could deliver in their civic lives and which subjects, on the other hand, they could recommend for promotion in the order. This degree, then, maintained the list of accommodations and directed the circulation of services. Since we now had the truest pictures of all external and internal qualities of our members before us, we knew of what use every one would be in the state. Therefore, we were in a in a position to only recommend the worthiest individuals, as is the duty of loyal citizens, instead of imposing our favorites onto the states at the expense of justice. We achieved what no monarch could do.

If a prince asked his minister who was an Illuminatus, "Whom do you think can I entrust with this position?" this minister could present his lord character profiles that enabled him to choose the original from among many, foreigners and citizens, which most closely matched his desires. This degree was at last wholly Masonic, as far as the ritual was concerned. The ceremonies were meaningful, without child's play, festive, and deeply moving to anyone who does not seek to close his soul to any sensory impressions of that sort.

All these degrees, as I have described them so far, have been published at the place of printing, Edessa (Frankfurt on the Main) under the title *The True Illuminatus*[xii], but I do not know by whom. They are exactly as I have described them by my own hand, and I challenge anyone to find anything therein that is dangerous or in conflict with the obligations of a Christian, honest man, and good citizen. I must also remind the reader that *The Improved System of the Illuminati*[xiii], published by Herr Weishaupt, contains essays with which I am not in the least familiar and which had not been introduced while I was a member of that society.

The Scottish Novitiate was followed by the Scottish Knight, or the degree of the directing

Illuminatus—this was the transition to higher Masonry, the Mysteries Class. Had one of our members reached this point, he certainly must have been convinced of our cause's goodness and the usefulness of our system. Thus, if someone was eager to do something useful and noble, if he had good and faithful intentions, he could no longer desire to leave us. He knew that he would not find anywhere in the world that which he found with us. If it was not the most perfect system for a secret society, we at least had the sincerest, most effective process of attaining it. We had the greatest willingness to adopt all good things we were still lacking. We were tolerant. We were detached from system-spirit. We were entirely selfless. Finally, we were a forward looking, secure institution working for the best of each and every individual in their moral, spiritual, and civic life. Here then, an active man seeking truth and justice found another field of activity. If he was wiser and better than we, he found us eager to accept him as our teacher and leader; if not, he could find instruction with us and did not need to seek elsewhere. Thus, if he was an *Illuminatus Major*, and he was still attached to other societies, it could be expected that he was either a man without principles or a secret spy. We therefore demanded from the candidate, before promoting him to the

Scottish Knight Degree, a loyalty test, a revers to the following effect: that from now on, he was to remain faithful to us, have no closer connection to any other order, and never resign. The reader will learn on the following pages that this oath was rescinded in the higher degrees, when we were at last sure of the man. In addition, it was immediately dispensed (especially in the case of good persons, who found this sort of restriction suspicious) on occasion. However, it was an excellent tool for removing those whom we did not fully trust, who did not adapt to our curriculum well, or those who, all our tests notwithstanding, had betrayed us. We thus presented these men with the oath and insisted on its execution. If they refused, they resigned without making a fuss, or they remained in the lower degrees. As the lesser Illuminati supervised the seed schools, so the Scottish knights directed the lesser Freemasonry of the three symbolic degrees, according to our plans, and they were instructed accordingly. At the same time, the Lodge Ritual or the Chapter on the Knights and the catechism for that degree hinted at the higher meaning of the Masonic hieroglyphs with the instruction to diligently contemplate these, to research them, and to report their thoughts to the superiors in these matters. Some would have at last tired in their cumbersome advance across this mystical terrain; perhaps, they would abandon their speculations and adhere to our other purposes, to actively work in the world. Other good people, conversely, whose ultimate goal was the so-called higher sciences and the study of these hieroglyphs and who seemed unsuitable for more refined activity and the highest offices of the order, could remain in this degree and I would have ensured that they would have received ample sustenance suited to their tastes. As far as the particular ritual of this degree is concerned, it did not at all fit into Herr Weishaupt's initial plan, as can be seen in the *Original Writings*; the whole matter was distasteful to him; he felt it was too religious, to quixotic, too theosophical. However, I would like to try to explain why, apart from the reasons I have already given, I designed the degree this way and not any other, so that I may add the following in my defense. First, I would like to remind the reader that anything of religious significance in these rituals, for example the Love feasts or Agapes, cannot be regarded as my inventions. They were taken from old, authentic Scottish Freemason rituals, and I intended to place their explanations, the result of arduous research that may have not so much displeased Herr Weishaupt after all, among the higher mysteries. One should further recall that I was dealing with all sorts of people, those who loved religion and those who hated it. I believed that in an order that sought to spread out in such a manner that it covered all things important and holy to men, its members should be in agreement as far as positive religion was concerned. It certainly wasn't the intention to create a general religious community, nor to introduce indifferentism, no! Everyone was to remain firm in his convictions and faithful to his established principles, but he was also to grant the same to his brothers, not to despise the doubters and the adherents of other religions, much less persecute them; to the contrary! he was to ascertain that the basis of all these various religious teachings lay in very simple truths which merely had been modified by circumscription and incorporation and only seemed to be different or contradictory to one another. I believed that my research, which I conducted by way of the old and new mystery schools, primarily Freemasonry, to have found the key to Christianity in certain hieroglyphs which had transitioned from one secret society to the next nearly unaltered. I have written about this topic more extensively in my *Contribution to the Latest History of the Order of Freemasons*[xiv], in the ninth conversation, beginning with page 172. According to my plan, these findings were to be found in the greater mysteries, and the Scottish rituals merely hinted at them. However, the following principles guided my steps in all this: human beings need a positive religion, even if God's revelation was nothing further than reason revealed, even if it taught nothing more what we would have discovered on our own, though later, through our own contemplations, as soon as the education of the human spirit had attained the highest degree. Thus the doctrine that the light of reason is sufficient to enlighten us about our obligations and to fulfill our current and future destiny with confidence and serenity, could only suit the wisest and the best. The great heap of mediocre people requires a higher authority for the truths it needs to follow. If it is allowed to build its system of theories on its mere raisonnement, it will be impeded in this effort to create a coherent and consistent system not only by its own lack of insight or it will regurgitate others that may not have a bona fide logical structure, but it will be blinded by its desires and passions. It will fashion a convenient theory sparing these passions, and by doing away with positive religion, it also destroys its morality—We learn this through the experiences gathered through the ages; it also teaches that even the wise need a positive religion.

Man doubts, searches, wishes, mainly to receive the light, as far as his condition after death is concerned. However, he does not wish to be filled with hope about it; rather, he wishes to have certainty about it. If he cannot attain this certainty through his intellect, he completely renounces his confidence in his own views, at last, preferring to believe the most distasteful drivel, running into the arms of charlatans and accepting the most ridiculous system as divine revelation, as long as it provides him with assurances regarding his future destination on the other side of the grave—This explains the strange phenomenon that the moment of enlightenment is usually followed by a period of the most atrocious superstition! Thus, men who hold the happiness and serenity of their brothers near to their hearts must therefore strive to maintain a proper balance between faith and reason and a positive religion that does not appear as being in conflict with rational thought to the scientist and, at the same time, soothes the weak, guides his morality, and warms his heart. Now, among all these positive religions there is none that so completely corresponds to this ideal as the Christian religion, purged of human statutes, and drawn directly and without perversion from the Bible. Thus it was important to work for the preservation of this religion, and do accomplish this, it seemed necessary:

1. To make it interesting and integrate it into our system by commemorating its divine founder through simple, moving ceremonies in our assemblies after the manner of the Scottish Rites Masons, representing Freemasonry (according to its own foundation) as a closer outcrop of better Christians.
2. It was proved that the Messiah's teachings proclaimed the highest truth and goodness, whose aim it was to execute an immensely great and noble plan for humanity, which was none other than the plan of our society and higher Freemasonry, and finally:
3. That even the secrets of the Christian religion did not contradict reason, but rather contained a most exalted philosophical meaning, but that understanding this meaning, which required diligent study, was neither useful nor necessary for all persons, that, in essence, the nature of this religion lay not in speculations, but the execution of its majestic teachings.

I tried to effect the first in the Scottish Knight degrees. The second could be found in the Lesser Priest degree. The third was to be the substance of the Greater Mysteries. Anyone who reads the

Scottish Knight degree can see that such were my intentions. I no longer possess any copies, and it is not in print. It contained, as I have mentioned above, a ritual celebrating the Agapes or Love Feasts in the manner of the first Christians. The sincerest, warm reverence for the Christian religion shone through all these things, and he who wishes to learn more about my religious principles, can read the three collections of sermons[29]. And if here and there, a few bold or careless expressions can be found in the *Original Writings*[30], it should not be forgotten that I had to adjust my tone a little to suit every person's disposition to execute the plan I had set out to fulfill. This plan may have been flawed—and it certainly was, as I later saw—but it certainly was well-intentioned, and if some dreamy enthusiasm was at play, this enthusiasm was so harmless that it rather spurred me on to work for the best interests of others.

---

[29] First collection: *Six Sermons About Despotism, Stupidity, Superstition, Injustice, Faithlessness, and Sloth*, Frankfurt on the Main by Andrea, 1783. Second collection: *Six Sermons About Humility, Gentleness, Inner Peace, Prayer, Charity, and Tolerance*, by Pfaehler in Heidelberg, 1786. Third collection: *Six Sermons About Consolation in Suffering, Taming the Passions, Good Works, Libel, Bible Study and Flattery,* by Andrea, 1788.

[30] For example, in the *Postscript*, bottom of page 205

Not even the smallest fees were charged for acceptance into all these degrees—Neither did we require coffers.—Where seed schools held assemblies, it was left up to the members to agree on how they were to bear the costs for postage and the like. Our Freemason Lodges were at liberty to determine and use their membership fees in the manner usual to the order, but they were obliged to offer an account to the Scottish Chapter. Not the least amount was sent to the higher chiefs, and money was not even spoken of in the Mysteries Class.

I shall now describe this Mysteries Class. The Lesser Mysteries encompassed the Priest and Regent Degrees.

If one would like to argue about words and tie the term Priest Degree to the hateful notion of parsimony, hierarchical institutions, Papist-Jesuit machinations that has rested upon it for quite some time, this title could indeed be suspicious to many a man. However, my understanding of a priest at the time was: the leader and interpreter of the people's religion; of the priest class: that class of citizens in a state which was to be regarded as the keepers of all knowledge important and sacred to humankind—in short! the Minervals were to be pupils and students; the Freemasons, educated, worldly men and businessmen; the priests, scholars and teachers; the regents, leaders and directors; and finally, the members of the Higher Mysteries degrees, speculative seers, who had withdrawn into a philosophical retirement after they had been active in the world long enough. I have already stated above, that this Priest Degree demonstrates how wise, comforting, and beneficial the teachings of Christ are, and what a great plan can be found therein. Because it was here, where the purpose of the divine Redeemer was examined: to raise humanity back to its original dignity; to raise morality to its highest degree through wise education; to introduce a general regimen of morals, so that anyone could remain faithful to virtuousness from his inner conviction that only virtue can bring happiness, without coercion; to bind all people to one another with the bonds of brotherhood; to remove all immediate conditions causing poverty, need, and the fight against depravity and immorality by enabling us to govern ourselves and consequently do without all artificial institutions, constitutions and positive laws. It was furthermore taught, and proved with passages from the Gospel, that true Christianity was not a popular religion, but a system for the chosen ones, that Jesus had communicated the higher purpose of his teachings only to his trusted apostles. And this, it was said, was propagated in its initial stages by the *disciplina arcani* among the first Christians, taught in dual fashion, exoteric and esoteric, in the mystery schools of the Gnostics, Manicheans, Ophists, etc., and then at last, after many other migrations, hidden in the hieroglyphs, became the property of the Order of Freemasons. A large part of these deductions stemmed from Spartacus himself, and this certainly was not his worst creation. This part can be found in the appendix to the *Postscript* under the title, "Section Two, Documents," page 80 ff.—Herr Weishaupt later intended to insert this essay into the degree of the directing Illuminati (which I referred to as the Scottish Knight degree)—and I believe one will not be able to deny one's own applause to the principles expressed therein. By the way, even the *Original Writings* prove that the Priest degree was considered great and important among our noblest members—and how could it have been otherwise? One only needs to read the pages to which I have just referred! Read them impartially and then judge for yourself, if they do not expound Christ's teachings from an exalted, attractive perspective. Certainly many will miss a few dogmatic sentences, which are nothing if not renounced, but are also not particularly taught at this juncture; however, one must also consider that this essay was not meant to be a theological compendium, that its main purpose was to represent religion from such a perspective that it would be interesting to all people, even unbelievers. Can one find fault in this purpose, when Herr Nicolai has recently stated, and that worthy, pious Zollikofer has declared, he saw no wrong in holding a Deist worship service in which all religious people could participate? The ceremonies I had prescribed for this degree seemed simplistic and insignificant to Herr Weishaupt[31]. It is known that he was prejudiced against anything of this kind. Meanwhile, I can assure the reader, that quite a few very reasonable men found these very ceremonies touching, dignified, and solemn. And by the way, I gladly admit that my old ideas of priesthood and initiation shone through all my work in the order, that my sanguine, melancholy temperament and a certain tendency for melancholy and dissatisfaction with the world moved me to place more value on external soul-stirring traditions than those persons would approve, who only act from the head and call upon their reason to aid them against all sensual impressions. But what is the use? Did the wise man find less meaning in the doctrine simply

---

[31] *Postscript to the Original Writings*, p. 94

because I clad it in a certain garment that was pleasing to him who marched to the same drummer as I did? Various sufferings had given me this tendency to religious zeal. I do concede that it is certainly wiser so seek in the strength of reasoning, in quiet devotion to God, faithful of the Highest Being's justice, in spite of all obstacles, and to oppose all misfortunes with steadfastness and prudence, wiser than to numb oneself with by sensual means or to escape into a world of dreams—but who can always be wise?—This much about the curriculum and the external institution of the Priest Degree! Their efforts were very important, and at one time, they promised us the most magnificent fruits for the world, as far as the sciences were concerned, to whom they were solely dedicated. For we have heard that every pupil had to enroll in a scientific discipline and dedicate his energy to it, and was, upon request, required to gather information and perform research in this discipline. The priest class in each province was now to direct these literary operations under the direction of their dean. Everything had been divided into faculties, for example: natural sciences, history, psychology, mathematical sciences, etc. A priest was always to remain at the head of such a faculty and maintain a subject catalog for his field, in which the most important new discoveries were recorded. If someone required explanation or help with any scientific endeavor and turned to a superior in this matter, then, if the problem could not be solved with the information in the subject catalog, all students in this discipline would have been tasked to gather information for their anonymous friend. The research results of several hundred friends could have been delivered to the requesting party without complaint or academic jealousy. He could have begun to work, where many brilliant minds would have given up, would have found the materials already assembled and prepared. The weaker would have become the teacher of the stronger, and by and by, the order would have come into possession of the rarest knowledge in all areas of scholarship which would have been kept in a depository out of which the world would have received as much as was deemed necessary for each age, with a keen eye on the need and the degree of enlightenment.

Finally, there was the Regent Degree. Apart from a few ceremonies (in which I certainly like to clothe everything), this degree entailed the most carefully metered instructions for all higher chiefs, that is the superiors of the Scottish Knights (Scottish Grand Masters, also called Local Chiefs), for the

Provincials, Inspectors, and National Chiefs. Those who wish to ascertain, whether or not these instructions were authored with wisdom, honesty, and consistency should read as an example the Provincial Instructions in Section 2 of the *Postscript of the Original Writings*, page 17 ff. However, the Regent Degree also included the following characteristic, according to my own specifications: for it has been stated that this class was charged with the general government of the entire matter and was to report to use Areopagites only regarding their endeavors and progress. I thus expected that those members which had been found worthy, after manifold trials, to be accepted into the Regent Degree, were the noblest, most enlightened – in a word! the best trained persons. And these consequently deserved to be wholly free persons, answering only to reason and the most intimately accepted truth. They must not view themselves as our machines, the tools of anonymous chiefs, and I held the belief, it was the duty of us, the Areopagites, to place ourselves in the position to find among them bold gainsayers should it ever occur to us to execute dangerous plans from behind the screen of anonymity. To this purpose, I had arranged the annulment of all obligations exacted by us, yes! even his initial oath which included the promise of secrecy; the tables of his relations, his autobiography, his character profile—in short! everything about him that we held in our possession, everything that would have made him dependent on us in a certain manner, delivered him into our hands, all this was returned to him.

He was then told, "You are now completely free. If you find a more perfect, useful institution in another society, greater purity of purpose, more certain means to attain them, a sphere of influence more worthy of you, and if you find the corps of your current brothers not inclined to adopt these in our midst, it is your duty to resign and to go where your head and heart find greater satisfaction. In no way do we claim a monopoly for us, but we strive to work for the world's benefit, which is done nowhere else with this degree of perfection and is yet so necessary. If you find our labors are useless, idle, or even dangerous, your hands are now untied, and it is your duty to destroy the entire edifice through public exposure and cast shame on folly, fraud, and malice. But if you are satisfied with us—discounting the faults of all human endeavors—your own zeal will drive you to remain a faithful contributor, and to contribute everything for the basis and perfection of this system—not to please us, but from a drive to serve humanity"—I mean, this provision alone should testify to the purity of our intentions.

The Greater Mysteries class had not been established, as I have already mentioned. The object of these labors was to be the experiences and traditions of everything that could only be found to be great, sacred, and important to humanity in the mysteries of religion and higher philosophy. Only twelve Areopagites and a member elected from their midst as their leader would have belonged to this class, and in the case of the departure of an Areopagite, one could have chosen one of the Regents to fill this position.—

This was the entire structure of the order! And now step forward he who can find anything therein that would have threatened true religion, civic happiness, and good morals! And I say more: he step forward who can name me a society that had paid attention to all these things and so diligently cared for the happiness of humanity and the world, to transform the Earth into a family household of a common father's happy children! If many things occurred under me that were unfeasible or chimeric, I beg patience my well-intentioned enthusiasm! If rhapsodizing shone through this, it certainly was the sort of rhapsodizing that warmed the heart and spurred it to do noble deeds. If one interjects that this machine could have been misused, one should not forget that this is the case with all institutions in the world, and that in our case, abuse was prevented as much as that was possible — — However, my apologia is not necessary for this, as the matter has spoken for itself.

When I had thus completed this system fully, I sent all booklets to Spartacus, so they could be submitted to the Areopagites for review, according to the agreement. It took a very long time until I received the slightest reply[32], and still it was very important to me to see the edifice built at last, so I could satisfy my people, to lift the incredible burden from my shoulders, which I had hitherto carried, to delegate it to properly instructed and installed superiors in the five circuits of Germany.

On occasion, some of us, Spartacus among them, were of the opinion, it would be better not to rush the correction of the degrees, but by and by add another passage to the existing material as we became more experienced. They cited the example of the Jesuits, whose constitution only attained its consistency in increments, until it had become a work whose smallest parts were solidly cemented

---

[32] *Postscript to the Original Writings,* middle of page 75

together. I, however, had grounds to make the following objections:

1. The Jesuits were the unchallenged rulers over their pupils. At any moment, they could change their constitution at will—One had to obey them blindly. However, the obedience and dutifulness of our people only rested on the consistency and methodic manner of our rules which never were at conflict with one another.

2. Based on Herr Weishaupt's word, I had promised the men whom I accepted into the order promised a fully established society. I had lost all faith, and the matter itself would lose respectability, if they realized we were still working on the establishing the system, that it was still so new that not even its history was proof of the security of our institutions.

3. Fulfilling the promises made in the lower degrees depended on the establishment of the higher ones. If pupils needed to be educated, there needed to be person who would do so. These needed to be properly instructed, and this could only occur when instructions could be issued concerning all principles, purposes, and methods—in short! there were frequent stagnations in matters of science, politics,

ethics, in all things, as long as the system was not completed in its core[33].

It truly seemed as if Spartacus was impressed by the force of these reasons, and since the Areopagites still hesitated to return the booklets with their annotations, Herr Weishaupt wrote to me, "The whole thing must not be held back by the slothfulness of these persons. Please institute these degrees as you have designed them without giving it a second thought."

Finally, the approval of the others arrived and I received clean copies of all degrees with Spartacus' signet of the order and cipher. However, it was found that the religious ceremonies of the Scottish Knight degree could not easily introduced in Catholic states without danger, and they stipulated that they be allowed to omit them, according to the circumstances—they approved of everything else.

Now, who was happier than I? I distributed my degrees as conscientiously as possible—I say: as possible, because it is already known from the previous pages that the order's rapid progress made it impossible to exercise all necessary precautions, since I had not been able to

---

[33] *Postscript to the Original Writings,* page 194

investigate and lead them on my own. In addition, the manifold deceits which had sadly occurred in Freemasonry, had made the members mistrustful, especially those in the Protestant Provinces, who were not accustomed to blind obedience and unconditional faith, so that on occasion, in order to keep an unquiet spirit from further spreading the seed of this mistrust and to convince him of the goodness of our cause, I was required to permit a person here and there a deeper insight into the system than he deserved—but such cases were few. I installed in all regions high, middle, and low superiors and created a geography of the order[34], and as proof that my choices were not entirely unhappy ones remains the fact that, when I later left the order, Spartacus kept all these men—except for one, I believe—at the head of this work, yes! even promoted them to higher positions.

Now I also took it upon myself to influence Freemasonry. The circular I sent to the lodges[35] at that time will show whether my intentions in so doing were noble or not. We began to form our own lodge, and in part, I also took it over, all the rather since it was now obvious that the efforts of

---

[34] Section 2 of the *Postscript to the Original Writings*, last page
[35] Ibid., page 133

the conference in Wilhelmsbad had been basically fruitless, and all seemed to proceed well. The higher degrees were accepted enthusiastically—even when here and there someone offered a small objection as far as individual passages were concerned—everyone was satisfied. I enjoyed my work, delegated all management tasks, and worked, wherever there was an opportunity, as a subordinate member, yes! I reported to my own subordinates whom I had elevated to chiefs, as can be seen in the reports printed in the *Original Writings*.

But if I expected that the other Areopagites would choose the same path and adhere to all points of this contract, I learned that the exact opposite was true. Spartacus could not forget the notion of being the general in charge. It did not seem to occur to him that the order was now a society of free men, that in truth, it was no longer his property, his work, and no one should be surprised by this or consider it a crime, if one considers his governing main ideas and how easily a sense of inner worth and true achievement can escalate into egotism[36]. No sooner were the degrees finished and introduced, than he without further ado presented

---

[36] *Postscript to the Original Writings*, top of page 34, page 80, and top of page 81

me with his own changes, additions and modifications and demanded that I pass these on to my subordinates. And as exquisite as all these things may have been, I most certainly had to protest them[37]. Not to mention, that it was counter to our solemn agreement, that it was extremely circuitous to rewrite the many cahiers distributed over all areas of Germany and to have them authenticated once more, that it would make a mockery of and disparage me and the order with the subordinates and discourage them.

So I presented the following to Herr Weishaupt, "It is known that such a number of regulations countermanding the previous ones is a sign of a weak government and the safest way to ensure never to see any of these regulations obeyed. A flawed system that is consistently enacted in all points is almost always worth more than one that is not solid, at all, or one that must be continuously patched up."

But these reasons made no impression on him. He insisted on his way of thinking, and I on mine, and now he began to cultivate the opinion that this Philo, whom he once praised to the heavens was

---

[37] *Original Writings*, bottom of page 376. *Postscript* to the same, pages 66, 67, 82 and bottom of page 88.

now the most crooked, most miserable character. He held me accountable for every little disagreeable thing that occurred in my provinces, which could not be avoided in a work that had been pieced together in this manner—That was his flaw! My flaw was that I did not begin to proceed with the gentleness against him that I should have used[38]. I was proud of my achievements on behalf of the order—I certainly was entitled to this—which without me would have remained a rather insignificant institution. The mutual bitterness became worse. On both sides, we found people who chose one party or the other, and they exchanged threats I had issued in the heat of the moment, giving Spartacus cause to mistrust me[39].

However, the arbitrary modifications to the degrees were not the only thing giving me cause to complain. I had never been able to approve of Herr Weishaupt's way of acting like a general, sovereign, or should I say: master of household and teacher of us all and especially the Areopagites, and he did not refrain from doing so now. Now he praised one of us to spur on the others, to follow his example. Now he chastised another to make this person understand the error

---

[38] *Postscript to the Original Writings,* page 92
[39] *Postscript to the Original Writings,* Pages 81 and 84

of his ways. Another time he declared he would no longer keep Mahomed informed, to punish him. And yet another time he wrote me from Athens he would let me go until I showed him obedience, etc.—One can understand that men do not like to put up with this sort of thing.

In addition, the other Areopagites did not fulfill their promise to surrender their leadership, but continued to run their Provinces arbitrarily. Nothing was done collaboratively, but unilaterally and arbitrarily.

Behind my back, Spartacus began to exchange letters with the chiefs I had installed and other individual members, letting them know in no uncertain terms that he was the founder and chief of the entire order. The new degrees were to be instituted here and there by these individuals. Since these differences in the distributed degrees made several people suspicious, the underhanded rumor was sewn that I must have perverted these degrees. The degrees sent from Bavaria were the genuine ones, since it was known that it was from there that it spread to our regions.

When the individual members with whom Herr Weishaupt had exchanged letters expressed opinions in their correspondence with which he agreed, when they decried superstition, folly, and slavery, when they spoke with affection and enthusiasm of his order and this great man, whom they did not know, from whose head had sprung such a brilliant plan, then they could convince this good man, Weishaupt, so new to the world and so zealous for the good cause, of anything. He allowed them to work in foreign Provinces. He listened to their banter without asking me whether they had any quarrel with that person or not when they said this man was the brightest mind, and that man was the most artless dreamer. Based on his applause, they then took liberties he never could have given them and of which he certainly knew nothing. They preached their personal opinions and presented them as the order's principles, used their pupils to persecute their personal enemies as enemies of the truth. In a certain region, books denouncing Christianity were publicly recommended to the Minervals. Among these, Horus was recommended. They joined issue with a certain—should I say scholar?—no! book writer who was known for his shameless quill as well as he was despised for his immoral lifestyle. They founded the Association of Eclectic Freemasons without my knowledge—in short! they acted so arbitrarily and against the contract terms and their promises that I was inundated with reproaches and complaints from all corners of Germany. I presented my position—one refused to listen to me. Everything I had done for the order was forgotten. Evil men, among them—it saddens me to say—many of whom were greatly indebted to me, incited Herr Weishaupt more and more against me. My nerves were stretched to the breaking point. I forgot myself to the point that I threatened to publish the history of this society in which one went about with such ingratitude and so much despotism. But one knew me too well, knew I was not capable of doing such a thing. Spartacus, who was general, was unable to abandon his way of thinking that he should forgive nothing, that he was able to discard any man, did not yield, but demanded submission. He challenged me to work against the order, now that I had given up all leadership. He mocked my powerlessness, assured me he had no further use for me and did not fear me. And since I had at the time had assumed the temporary supervision of a small district that was not yet in order, Herr Professor Weishaupt had forgotten our relationship to the extent that he delivered me orders through one of my former subordinates I had installed as a chief that were formulated as instructions one would have sent to a school boy.

Although this said much of Spartacus' steadfastness and consistency by setting aside everything his reason and heart certainly would have told him when it came to the dignity of the cause, which he was not willing to sacrifice, one can certainly imagine how much this must have upset me. This was exacerbated by the fact that gradually, very disparaging rumors regarding my actions against the order began to spread everywhere, and I had to suffer a thousand badinages from insignificant persons. Still, I did not proceed without restraint. I wrote to the Areopagites and asked them for help and advice[40]. I wrote to Spartacus with a peace offering[41]. The former asserted I was in the right, but later changed their minds. The latter, on the other hand, did not reply at all. I proposed a new convention to settle all differences. Spartacus thwarted it[42]. Now, however, I believed I owed it to myself and others who might suffer this fate, at least the best men among the brothers, to make the whole story of these dealings known. I mailed and handed some of these men an essay, in which I described everything briefly, and I certainly was

---

[40] *Postscript to the Original Writings*, page 99
[41] Ibid. page 118
[42] *Postscript to the Original Writings*, page 385

not trying to prevent anyone from making copies of this essay.

In the meantime I began to fear I could be tempted to commit an act of base vengeance—my lively temper, my insulted honor, my injured pride—all these stirred me up. I was convinced I had to prevent this. I had a great number of letters by Spartacus and others in my possession, whose publications would have gravely embarrassed many a man. One day, I burned the greatest part of these letters and sent the others back to the concerned parties. I gifted the cahiers of all the degrees to a conscientious and discreet Freemason who in exchange certified he would not misuse them. The files concerning an important matter of business which was of grave importance at a great court, with which I had been entrusted when the brothers' faith in me had been at its highest, but which had never left my possession and of which I had never written to Bavaria, I returned to the great prince whom the matter concerned. He accepted them very graciously, and if he did not permit me to use his name, it was not without his consent that I speak of this very fact.

At last, several honorable men at the head of the national order, to whom I had opened my heart, were moved to create a settlement, effective July 1,

1784, so that the matter would not escalate and to avoid worse consequences. The terms were as follows:

1. I would receive a written document, signed and sealed with the legal names and signets of two high ranking, honorable members, according to their social standing, philosophy, and offices within the order, containing the following: it was attested that I withdrew from the order voluntarily, and that my former zeal in the proliferation of the order was acknowledged with gratitude. This document is still in my possession, and I can present it, if necessary.
2. It was promised that a circular would be sent to all brothers, beginning with the lesser Illuminatus degree that would put to rest all derogatory and false rumors regarding my conduct in the order, and forthwith order them all to leave me in peace.
3. I would return all order documents still in my possession and bound myself to observe silence with respect to everything that had occurred, not to work against the philanthropic intentions of the order, and neither to name nor compromise its chiefs.

I have kept my part of this bargain faithfully and conscientiously, regardless of the fact that I was asked to speak about this on many occasions. I have kept quiet until now, despite the fact, that as I would and did say everything published was done so out context and in part presented to the public in a very false light. I have remained silent despite the fact that the *Original Writings* seemed to cast grave suspicions against me, first, because they portrayed me as one of the first chiefs of a society accused of having dangerous intentions, and second, because Herr Weishaupt's printed letters to the Areopagites could cast my own conduct in the order in a dubious light, as far as many a profane person, yes! even many a member of the order was concerned. I have kept my word. I regret to say that the good intentions of these two exalted brothers were not completely fulfilled by the others. Much ignoble badinage by certain individuals created many evil hours for me. Some of the mid-level chiefs neglected to inform the others of the circular which was to prove my innocence, while others dragged their feet until they were repeatedly ordered to do so. When the persecution in Bavaria commenced, there were evil persons, who, until their motives became generally known, underhandedly spread the rumor, I had been led by a desire for revenge and actively assisted in this matter. Finally, when the essay I mentioned above, which I had written in my own defense and in a closed compact delivered to many a brother, was still circulating here and there, and some of my friends, who knew of the further course of events and told the story of my quarrel with Spartacus with more affection that wisdom, I was held accountable for that, as well—but I have overcome all these things. Time has healed many wounds, and I can attest in good conscience, that since July 1. 1784, I have not had the least, remotest interest in anything concerning the Order of Illuminati, be it good or ill: whether it has continued, or still does, in this or another form, whether new degrees have been adopted and what their nature may be, whether Spartacus and the other Areopagites have remained at the head, whether or not the Bavarian brothers gave cause for the government's speedy and strict proceedings against them; who dreamed up all these intrigues to begin with—Indeed, I know nothing at all about any of these things, and I have purposely avoided discussing them even with my closest friends. I have renounced all activity with secret societies, and I have published this credo[43]. The only exception to this is that, as a favor, I assumed an office in a Heidelberg Freemason lodge, when it was established, where I undertook the labor of

---

[43] In my above mentioned writings: *On Human Relations*, etc.

writing its constitution.—And that also is a testament of my impartiality, because that lodge mainly followed the resolution of the Wilhelmsbad Congress—

One cannot begrudge me that I speak at last, and for the last time, about this matter, now that everyone has the published original writings in his hands and I have been publicly named, since, on the other hand, my prolonged silence could be interpreted as malicious, now that nearly all other interested parties have made public appearances.

If I have been too partial, perhaps praised myself too much, if I presented my own cause too one-sidedly and in too favorable a light, I ask that I be forgiven for this! Which son of the earth is completely impartial where his own cause is concerned, and who is wholly free from vanity?

Other than the published documents and the ones I have previously mentioned, I do not have any others which could attest to the truthfulness of my statements. Whether my friends have kept such documents and would be willing to present them, if necessary, that is another question. But I challenge him to step forward who could prove that I have made a single false pretense in these pages, whose main contents I would be able to affirm under oath, if the matter were important enough.

Endnotes:

---

[i] Gabriel-Louis-Calabre, *L'Ordre des Francs-Maçons Trahi et le Secret des Mopses Revelé*. 1742

[ii] in present-day Switzerland

[iii] *Allgemeines System für das Volk zur Grundlage aller Erkenntnisse für Menschen aus allen Nationen, Ständen und Religionen, 1778*

[iv] Anonymous, *Der Stein des Anstossess und der Fels der Aergerniss.* 1780

[v] Francois Louis de Beyerle

[vi] *Beytrag zur neuesten Geschichte des Freymaurer-Ordens, 1786*

[vii] Louis-René de Caradeuc de La Chalotai (1701-1785), French jurist, ardent opponent of the Jesuits

[viii] Ueber Jesuiten, Freymaurer und teutsche Rosencreutzer (1781)

[ix] Salutem plurimam dicit (many greetings)

[x] *Die Verirrungen des Philosophen, oder die Geschichte von Ludwig von Seelberg (1787), Ueber den Umgang mit Menschen (1788), Die Geschichte Peter Claussens (1783-1785)*

[xi] 1782

[xii] Johann Heinrich Faber, *Der Aechte Illuminat.* 1788

[xiii] *Das Verbesserte System der Illuminaten*, Adam Weishaupt, 1787

[xiv] *Beytrag zur neuesten Geschichte des Freymaurer-Ordens, in 9 Gespraechen, 1786*

Made in the USA
Middletown, DE
26 November 2017